ADELE

THE
OTHER
SIDE

AMY MACKELDEN

 **EYEWEAR** PUBLISHING

First published in 2016
by Eyewear Publishing Ltd
Suite 38, 19-21 Crawford Street
Marylebone, London W1H 1PJ
United Kingdom

Typeset with graphic design by Edwin Smet
Author photograph by Laura Hol
Adele 2009 picture with microphone Christopher Macsurak *(Creative Commons license)*
Printed in England by T J International Ltd, Padstow, Cornwall

ISBN 978-1-908998-91-0

Eyewear wishes to thank Jonathan Wonham for his very generous patronage of our press.

WWW.EYEWEARPUBLISHING.COM

For Mum & Dad

CONTENTS

INTRODUCTION

Who is this Adele person, exactly?

If you've picked up this book, chances are you know exactly who Adele is. How could you not? After all, this is a singer-songwriter who sold in excess of 800,000 copies of her new album *25* in its first week in the UK alone. And as for Adele's music video for recent single 'Hello', it had over "27.7 million views in its first 24 hours"[1]. To top it all off, Adele achieved it all with minimal marketing, barely using social media, and having been largely absent from the public eye for several years. Well played, Adele, well played.

If, for some unknown reason, you've managed to avoid finding out anything about Adele, I envy you. I'm kidding. You must live a very sheltered life, and thank goodness you have acquired this book so you could find out all about the current Queen of Pop. It appears that Adele has usurped all others – Taylor Swift, Katy Perry, Madonna – to be victoriously dubbed the only member of music royalty worth caring about. So how exactly has she done it?

Adele was born on 5 May 1988. In *The Telegraph* in 2008, at the start of her career, Stuart

Husband said, "Adele's back story is a study in tenaciousness. She was born in Tottenham, North London, to an 'arty mum', whom she describes as a 'trained masseuse, an artist, and a furniture-maker' (hence, perhaps, Adele's distinctive middle names)";[2] her full name is certainly unusual: Adele Laurie Blue Adkins, which gives other current celebs a run for their money. Adele's mother was supportive of her daughter's musical ability from an early age, and "encouraged the soul singer to test her limits and explore her creative side," Kate Beaudoin writes for *Mic*.[3] It's unsurprising to read that Adele showed promise from early on in her life, and as Beaudoin says:

> From four years old, Adele had been obsessed with emotive voices, especially those of singers like Mary J. Blige, Lauryn Hill and Alicia Keys. But her real musical 'awakening' came when she discovered Etta James and Ella Fitzgerald records at a thrift store.[4]

As Adele's British, she'd probably say 'charity shop', but it's true that she often cites Etta James and Ella Fitzgerald as responsible for her musical awakening.

This musical self-education that Adele went through seems to have impacted the style she's developed throughout her career. Her fascination with voices and the degree to which she was invested in the artists she grew up listening to prove that becoming a singer was the only legitimate career choice for Adele Adkins. As an avid Emma Bunton fan, Adele was keen to go to the Sylvia Young Theatre School, but as she said in an interview with *The Telegraph*, "my mum couldn't afford it".[5] However, not attending Sylvia Young doesn't seem to have hurt Adele's career prospects, and her talent didn't go unnoticed for long. As an alternative to Sylvia Young, Adele got a place at the BRIT School, which is free to attend. While most performing arts schools are quite costly, the BRIT school is part-funded by the British government. Because of its affordability, places at the school can be quite hard to come by, and the admissions process is renowned for being tough on applicants. For 14- to 19-year-olds, the school provides a comprehensive arts programme, which obviously works given the impressive alumni who have graduated from it: other famous alumni include Leona Lewis, FKA Twigs, Imogen Heap, Amy Winehouse, The Feeling, and Rizzle Kicks.[6]

Jessie J even mentions hanging out with Adele at the BRIT School in her autobiography, *Nice To Meet You*. Jessie J said, as quoted on

Capital FM, "I had all sorts of friends. I knew Adele; we were in the same year. We used to hang out at lunchtimes and have a little jam. We'd sing songs we'd written or perform whatever we were working on."[7] So many famous artists were nurtured at the BRIT School, and it's crazy to hear them talk about each other as old acquaintances in the playground. In February of 2013, *The Croydon Advertiser* said, "Adele joined the BRIT School... in Year 10 after spending three years at Chestnut Grove school in Balham, South West London. Miss Penney, who is head of music at the Brit, said Adele showed talent in her early years but that in Year 13 she started to become, 'more noticeable as someone who could write and sing'."[8]

Adele said of her education, "The BRIT School was cool. The kids were passionate about what they were doing there, whereas the ambition at my state school was to get pregnant and sponge off the government. That ain't cool."[9]

Adele was keen to forge her own career and earn her own money, and being around likeminded students helped her achieve that goal. Having the opportunity to specialise in her chosen subject early in her academic career, as well as hone her performance skills, laid the foundations for Adele's persona. And despite having a love of old records,

Adele knew that the internet was the way forward for music (somewhat ironically, considering her recent move to refuse streaming of her third album, *25*). In 2008, Adele told Stuart Husband in *The Telegraph*, "The BRIT teachers were a bit out of touch. I tried to teach them a bit about the internet, but they seemed to think everyone bought records and stuff."[10] Not only is this is a hilarious comment, following Adele's own statement about her own rejection of streaming services in favour of physical copies, it shows that Adele has always been acutely aware of trends among music lovers. She's an incredibly savvy artist, and seemingly has been since the very beginning of her career, understanding the ways in which people buy, listen to, and share music. Adele graduated in May 2006[11], and what happened next had a great deal to do with her online presence.

So without further ado, how was Adele discovered?

Adele's story starts the way in which many modern day success stories start – on Myspace. Justin Bieber may have been discovered on YouTube, but Adele's music was uploaded to Myspace by a friend, and the rest is history. It's an exciting tale for aspiring artists everywhere; the internet has allowed people to share their work like never before, and if the most successful singer in the world right now was found this way, then surely you can be too. Well, not on Myspace, because no one uses that anymore, right? Stuart Husband writes that Adele was signed "in November 2006, on the strength of three songs uploaded on her MySpace page."[12] Adele had caught the attention of XL, an independent record label, who must be incredibly glad they signed the singer as early on as they did. According to *The Telegraph*, "Adele...first had to book a gig at a Brixton pub to prove it really was her singing."[13] Whether this is true, or merely legend, Adele exploited the fact that the internet was the future of the music industry (despite, more recently, denying this very fact), and caught the attention of important music industry people by using her biggest asset: her voice. The singer has discussed the internet a great deal, particularly in her earliest interviews, telling Husband, "It's a great way of getting stuff out there. I'd much rather five million people heard my music, than I earned £5 million."[14] As an artist, Adele started out humble, and keen to generate an audience, and was much less concerned with the financial side of the industry. While this has changed, it's still true that

Adele's focus in firmly on the music, as evidenced by her refusal to model or take on any commercial sponsorships or endorsements. It's inevitable that an artist as famous as Adele would want to take control of the financial side of her business, but it's a marked change from the fresh-faced artist interviewed by *The Telegraph* in 2008 who said she'd blown all of her million-pound advance for album *19* on "Burberry and account cabs".[15] I miss this early career Adele, making elaborate purchases, not at ease with her fame and still living at home with her mum. That's the version of Adele I can get on board with, and it's surely the same Adele that fans fell in love with early on. The Adele who wanted people to hear her music, who didn't insist on people only having access to her songs following a cash transaction.

The Telegraph said, "The first song Adele ever wrote was a stirring, acoustic folk anthem, 'Hometown Glory', when she was 16."[16] That 'Hometown Glory' went on to be such a major hit for Adele is incredibly impressive considering she was so young when she wrote it. Adele has clearly always had an ear for a hit, and a capability for writing honest, catchy lyrics which her audience can connect with immediately. While Adele has always been candid, early in her career she was much more outspoken than the Adele we see in 2016. Her previous openness is endearing.

Tom Lamont, a writer in *The Guardian*, has an inside insight into Adele that many others don't, having seen her perform at the start of her career, and then interviewing her in the lead-up to the release of *25*. Describing early Adele, Lamont said she was, "Cooler-than-you cool, a fringed teenager who went around behind aviators and Marlboro smoke, whose friends were mostly striving artists, who kept in her bag a copy of *Time Out* folded to the gigs page. When I first saw Adele perform, at a small London show back in 2007, she came on stage wearing a floral frock and a snarl. She played an acoustic guitar while drinking a pint."[17] While it feels as though this version of Adele is mostly gone now, replaced by designer clothes and professionally applied make-up, it's great to hear these comparisons from someone who's followed her career from the very start. It's hard to imagine 2016 Adele drinking a pint while she performs on stage, and the cigarettes are long gone now, too. People may have forgotten Adele's previous incarnations, but she's a chameleon, a subtly evolving superstar.

Describing Adele in *The Telegraph* in 2011, Neil McCormick said, "She swears like a particularly foul-mouthed trooper. Transcribing her quotes, I generally have to cut out a word from every other sentence." Adele's coarse, unedited Britishness has always endeared her to the general public, and Americans particularly enjoy her accent. Sure, the swear words seem to have been replaced with Jackie O sunglasses and black-and-white music videos in which Adele drinks from porcelain cups of tea, but I like to think that that first version of Adele, the one introduced to the world on Myspace, by way of the BRIT School, is the real one. She may only exist in old interview snippets and article clippings, but under the now incredibly stylised exterior, I know that the old Adele is still there, desperate for a smoke, interspersing words with swears, ready to take on the world, and simultaneously unprepared for the success that is to follow.

PART 1

LISTENING TO ADELE IN PUBLIC, CRYING

Tell me about her albums.

<u>About *19*</u>

Adele's first album, *19*, was released in January 2008, and an early review for the BBC by Chris Long said of her, "It's easy to get the wrong impression about Adele. She looks like another Kate Nash, all Topshop dresses and haircuts that only a mother could love. And the fact that she's been a fuss on Myspace only ups the sense of trepidation."[18] This isn't the only time Adele was compared to Nash. *Slant Magazine* said, "Critics have favourably compared Adele to Amy Winehouse, but most of *19* plays like the quieter moments on Kate Nash's *Made of Bricks*... Adele's vocals are richer than Nash's, though, and Joss Stone would be a better point of reference."[19] *The Guardian*'s Caspar Llewellyn Smith said, "First picked as one to watch in this magazine exactly 12 months ago, along with Kate Nash... Adele could have since then papered her bedroom with all the hype."[20] Excitement was building for Adele long before her first album came out, which shows that, as an artist, she's always been capable of generating interest in her material; it seems as though Adele was destined for greatness long before she released any music. That she was compared to other ingénues of the time is no surprise. After all, every magazine is ever ready to name the new "Radiohead". But the fact that Adele has stuck around long after many of her contemporaries' own careers have fizzled out is a true testament to her talent.

Some of the reviews for *19* are worth examining because it seems as though not everyone could tell Adele was going to be the huge success she's gone on to be. It's endearing that Adele's understated look and sound didn't prepare the general public for the astronomical star she was due to become. Long at the *BBC* said, "*19* is a great start, a solid base to build a career on and a wonderful reminder of just how great our home-grown talent can be."[21] While Long's praise certainly pre-empts the general hysteria that was to follow *19*'s release, he's also incredibly cautious with the compliments he gives to the singer, and is pensive about whether she will actually be able to live up to expectation. Reading back his review from 2008, it seems as though Long could see that Adele had skill, but also the potential to crash and burn. Interestingly, the *BBC* review notes that Adele's "voice lacks a little soul and her songwriting a little depth."[22] Considering the accolades Adele has been consistently racking up since 2008, it seems as though the public firmly disagree with this opinion, though it's natural to question any new artist and wonder whether they have the staying power required to make it in the music industry.

Adele released four singles from *19* in 2008[23] ('Hometown Glory' first came out on 7" Limited Edition Vinyl through Pacemaker Recordings in 2007[24], but was re-released in 2008 and had far more success). 'Hometown Glory' became an instant anthem for British people everywhere, because of its lyrical fondness for the place Adele grew up. 'Chasing Pavements' is still one of Adele's most iconic songs, and it counts high-profile celebrities like Simon Cowell amongst its fans. 'Cold Shoulder' and Bob Dylan cover 'Make You Feel My Love' were also released as singles.

It was the subtlety of Adele's debut that resonated with listeners everywhere. Sure, Adele garnered critical acclaim right from the very start, but it was the ease with which she dropped *19*, a mature-sounding debut by all measures, that started gathering her fans right from the early days.

As *The Guardian* said, "Rather than screaming for attention, there's an artistically focused stillness at the centre of so many of these bruising love songs."[25] Adele's first album may have been understated, but that was one of its main strengths. By showcasing her potential, and launching material when she was ready, Adele created strong foundations upon which to begin building her empire. Looking back, it seems as though Adele was firmly in control of her journey from the very beginning.

About *21*

Something pretty spectacular happened in March of 2015. It was announced that Adele had achieved a completely impressive feat: *The Guardian* wrote, "Adele's *21* has sold more copies in the UK than any other album this millennium."[26] This put Adele's album ahead of Amy Winehouse's *Back To Black*, and ahead of albums by James Blunt, Dido, Michael Bublé, and Coldplay. To come out on top proves that Adele's impact has always been quite stunning. While Adele's album *19* makes the Top 30 Bestselling Albums of the Millennium, it's *21* that claims the top spot, with its sophomore superiority, raw confidence, and endless accessibility.[27]

Following the huge success of *21*, Neil McCormick wrote in *The Telegraph*, "These are rarefied heights for an artist, when their music enters the realms of cultural ubiquity, crossing all borders, satisfying all tastes, to exist everywhere at the same time." If *19* could be referred to as a popular album, *21* was something else altogether. It seemed to inspire a mild hysteria in the general public that little else had managed to before or has since. In fact, the unprecedented level of success that *21* garnered left Adele shell-shocked and creatively blocked. As she said in a profile in *The New York Times*, "I didn't think I had it in me to write another record. I didn't know if I should. Because of how successful *21* was, I thought, 'Maybe everyone's happy with that being the last thing from me. Maybe I should bow out on a high.'"[28] While Adele has since proven this fear completely untrue, it's funny to hear the singer-songwriter feel as though she may have reached the end of her career at such an early age. Having released an album so ubiquitous, Adele was understandably stunted, unsure how or if she could follow it up. Sure, her fans had more faith than that, and knew that there was much more to come post-*21*, an album which was both immensely satisfying yet also left everyone wanting more.

Adele has spoken at length about the process of writing *21*, and the massive highs and lows that went with it. In *The New York Times*, Adele said,

> I just used to let myself drown. If I was sad, if I was confused – which I would say were the running themes for most of my records so far – I'd just go with it. I'd let myself fall apart, and I'd sit in darkness, and I'd feel sorry for myself, and I wouldn't accept any help to get out of it... I loved the drama of it all.[29]

While the depth of these emotions is evident throughout Adele's second album, the process of writing and recording it sounds gruelling, and not something anyone would want to repeat. While it paid off, and Adele's incredibly personal songs meant that a wide-ranging audience connected with, and fell in love with, songs like 'Someone Like You', it makes sense that as a human being, she wouldn't want to visit one of the most painful times of her life. As Adele said, "How I felt when I wrote *21*, I wouldn't want to feel again. It was horrible. I was miserable, I was lonely, I was sad, I was angry, I was bitter. I thought I was going to be single for the rest of my life. I thought I was never going to love again."[30] While the product of Adele's sadness has proved to be a musical classic and monumental bestseller, as well as an album her fans return to again and again, the writing and recording of it feels like an era she has very much put to bed. Sure, *25* deals with heartbreak, but there's a very real sense that Adele has moved on as an adult, understanding her self-worth, and refusing to undervalue who she is anymore.

The *New York Times* also noted the fact that Adele's life has changed immeasurably post *21*, and that now she's part of a family unit, she refuses to be as self-indulgent as perhaps she was before. On that very topic, Adele said, "I haven't got time to fall apart. I'm the backbone for my kid, and I want to be there for him. And I want to be there for my boyfriend as well, and I don't want to bring them down with me for my art."[31] Adele was clearly in the midst of a traumatic stage of her life during album *21*, but that's now changed dramatically. In some ways, music isn't the thing she puts first now, and that's not a criticism. It sounds as though, previously, Adele put music even before her own wellbeing. Sure, it was a way of exploring and understanding her emotions, but her approach to writing and recording now sounds much healthier. Music is definitely a priority of Adele's, but it's not the only one. The all-consuming sense of heartbreak and misery that Adele has said she went through while making *21* is totally evident on the record itself. It's an event, a marker, a captured moment in time. But it's 100% a good thing that Adele has moved on to a generally much happier place now.

Adele released five singles from *21*. 'Rolling In The Deep' was the first single from the album, released towards the end of 2010[32], with 'Someone Like You', 'Set Fire To The Rain', 'Rumour Has It', and 'Turning Tables' all released in 2011.

Kate Beaudoin did some important mathematics in her analysis of Adele's second album, writing for *Music.Mic* in June 2015, that:

> *21* spent an astonishing 23 weeks at No. 1 and to date has sold 4,751,000 copies in the UK. That's especially amazing when you consider that the UK only has a population of 64 million – meaning that enough copies were sold that nearly 15% of the entire country could own the album.[33]

It's pretty amazing to consider that as many as 15% of people in the UK might own a copy of Adele's *21*. Adele's reach is incredible when considered in these terms, and goes to show just how phenomenal her success really is.

The success of *21* was only hindered slightly by Adele's health issues; problems with her vocal chords forced Adele to cancel tour dates, and there seemed to be a real fear that if Adele didn't look after her throat, her singing career might be in jeopardy. Despite her cancellations, fans continued to stay committed to Adele, sending her well-wishes, and looking forward to any new material she might release in the future.

About *25*

Adele's long-awaited follow-up to *21* was met with generally positive reviews, and major fan praise. Writing in *The Guardian*, Alexis Petridis, said:

> There's something curiously irrelevant about reviewing Adele's third studio album... The public seems even less interested in critical opinion than usual, if such a thing is possible. It has already been taken as read that *25* is a masterpiece: its quality isn't up for question.[34]

This was one of the more honest write-ups, which acknowledged that Adele's fans weren't interested in analysis of the album, only the fact that they finally had access to it. It was Petridis's review which seemed to say all of the things that others didn't: Adele's music is still very much dealing with heartbreak, that the sound isn't that removed from her previous work, and that fans will be getting exactly what they expect with this new release. As Petridis said:

> No one who buys it is going to angrily return it to the shop because it wasn't what they expected. For the most part, *25* sticks close to the formula of the best-known tracks on its predecessor, *21*: big, piano-led ballads, decorated with strings and brass, dealing with heartbreak."[35]

Perhaps the secret to Adele's success is her understanding of what fans want, which overwhelmingly seems to be more of the same.

Topically, *25* doesn't seem to veer far from *19* and *21*. Speaking of *25*, Amanda Petrusich in *Pitchfork* said:

> Her third album concerns itself with the passage of time: the inevitable accumulation of both years and vantages. It's as if she knows intimately the nauseating experience of waking up one morning, surveying a half-lived life, and thinking, 'Oops.'[36]

This hilarious summation was one of the major criticisms Adele has continued to face with her material – that her lyrics often suggest a much old speaker, one who sounds as though near the end of their life, remembering things that happened in youth, and reflecting on years gone by.

In *The Guardian*, Petridis discussed how Adele's subject matter in *25* doesn't vary much from her previous material, still appearing to circle the heartbreak she experienced throughout *21*. Discussing the tracks on *25*, Petridis said:

> Most of them seem to deal with exactly the same heartbreak that fuelled *21*: five years on, Adele is still, metaphorically speaking, planted on her ex's lawn at 3 am, tearfully lobbing her shoes at his bedroom window.[37]

While Adele vehemently denies that she's writing about the same heartbreak as before, initial single 'Hello' evidences that the music is very recognisable. Saying that *25* has a completely different tone from her previous work isn't enough to make it true. If the songs sound like they're break-up anthems, even if that wasn't the intention behind them, surely that's exactly what they are?

In *Pitchfork*, Petrusich said:

> Lyrically, Adele leans on a familiar kind of outrage, reckoning with a lover who broke

every promise he ever made to her. There's unrequited love, but then there's love that changes shape; if you're unlucky enough to be on the receiving end of that transaction – made unwilling witness to the mysterious, alchemical shift in which devotion suddenly thins, sours – true understanding is impossible, a fool's errand.[38]

While love in different forms is an interesting variation on Adele's old work, as many of the songs appear to still address an old, jilted lover, *25* isn't necessarily the departure Adele keeps promising. Still, this appears to be what the fans want, and Adele certainly understands what her fans want if the sales of *25* are anything to go by. Though it begs the question: why deny that the album is about the very subjects that listeners believe it to be about? Surely, art is in the eye of the beholder, after all? Or in the ear of those who pay your bills.

Not all critics approached *25* with a critical edge, however. Neil McCormick wrote in *The Telegraph*, "What it sacrifices in youthful rawness it makes up in maturity and sheer class. Adele Adkins has taken her time over her third album and it shows."[39] Awarding the album five stars, McCormick was consistently impressed with Adele's new material, and the fact that it trod old ground was, in his opinion, a great thing. Even if the tone shift was only subtle, there have been many references to the "maturity" of Adele's third album. McCormick was particularly complimentary throughout his review: "The beauty of Adele's singing is how effortless it is. The depth of her notes is luxurious with the slightest of croaks in her upper range lending a twist of soul."[40] Adele's effortlessness, the ease with which she sings in a way that others can't, is part of the reason the public are so drawn to her. She's a safe pair of hands, and has the ability to make a binned receipt sound like poetry. Adele's music may be simple in its composition, and ever-accessible, but this is what makes it so popular. The slick production of *25* doesn't hurt either, and listening to the album will make you feel as though you're in on a global cultural event, one that's impossible to miss.

While 'Hello' is the only single to be released from *25* so far, it's been largely speculated that 'When We Were Young' would be the follow-up, especially as a version Live At Church Studios was uploaded to YouTube in November 2015.[41] Billboard cites a source at Columbia Records as confirming that 'When We Were Young' would be the second US single from *25* to be released.[42] Following the amazing success of 'Hello' as a single (it achieved platinum sales in the UK after only three weeks, by selling over 600,000 copies[43]), whichever song is picked as the second single from *25* is sure to do well.

Has Adele won any awards?

This is a ridiculous question. Adele has won *plenty* of awards, and shows no signs of stopping. Here's a run down of the crucial accolades:

Academy Awards

Most notably, perhaps, Adele has an Oscar. At the February 2013 ceremony, Adele took home the award for Best Original Song for her song 'Skyfall', theme to the James Bond movie of the same name.[44]

American Music Awards

In 2011, Adele won three AMAs, for Favourite Adult Contemporary Artist, Favourite Pop/Rock Female Artist, and Favourite Pop/Rock Female Album. In 2012, she won the award for Favourite Adult Contemporary Artist for a second time.[45]

Billboard Music Awards

Adele has won 13 Billboard Music Awards to date, and this number is sure to increase rapidly following the release of *25*.[46] Quite an impressive number for a Brit.

BRIT Awards

Adele won her first BRIT Award early in her career, taking home the Critics' Choice Award in 2008, and making some people wonder if the hype surrounding Adele was too high to live up to (it wasn't). In 2012, she won British Female Artist and British Album Of The Year.[47] In 2013, 'Skyfall' took home British Single Of The Year, and in 2016 she's nominated for four awards.

Adele's performance of 'Someone Like You' at the 2011 BRIT Awards propelled the album track (which wasn't due for release as a single for quite some time) to the top of the charts. *The Telegraph* wrote that the song, "a stripped down song about lost love, shot up from outside of the Top 40 to dislodge Jessie J from the number one slot."[48] While the BRIT Awards always increase the sales of performing artists and award-winners, it's unprecedented for a singer to steal the number-one spot that week with a song they've not yet released as a single. This was the start of Adele's cosmic climb to stardom.

Golden Globe Awards

'Skyfall' proved popular again, winning Adele Best Original Song at the Golden Globe Awards in 2013. Hollywood certainly beckoned.

Grammy Awards

Adele has been nominated for 13 Grammy Awards to date, and won ten. She took home six trophies in 2012 alone for her album *21* and its related singles.[49] You have to admit, that's more than a little impressive!

Ivor Novello Awards

Having been nominated for five Ivor Novello Awards during her career, for songwriting, Adele has so far won two, both in 2012.[50]

Mercury Prize

Although Adele has never won the Mercury Prize,

both *19* and *21* were nominated for it, in 2008 and 2011, respectively.

<u>MTV Video Music Awards</u>

Adele's work has collected three VMAs so far, all in 2011 for 'Rolling in the Deep', including Best Art Direction, Best Cinematography, and Best Editing.[51]

Is Adele obsessed with her age (*19*, *21*, *25*)? And why aren't her albums named after her age at the time they're released?

In an interview with *Beats1* host Zane Lowe, Adele discussed her use of her age in the titles of her albums. She said, "I was 20 when *19* came out. I was 23 when *21* came out. I am 27. And so proud of being 27… But I quite liked it when I was 25."[52] The fact that the albums are named after the age she was when she wrote them, rather than her age when each was released, has certainly confused some fans, particularly as *25* was released so soon after Adele's 27th birthday. But the titles appear to function as diary markers: the events contained in the songs on each record represent a year in Adele's life – not the year the album was released, but the year it was made. Like time capsules, *19*, *21*, and *25* each feature events, secrets, individuals, and changes that have taken place and have affected Adele at a particular time in her life.

Asked whether she would continue to name her albums after her age, Adele said, "I think this will be my last age one. I'm sure I'm wrong with this but I feel there's been a massive change in me in the last couple of years."[53] While she cannot be certain of this yet, and has made jokes to the contrary already, it feels as though Adele is closing a chapter with *25*, moving on from the relationships which used to define her, and becoming much more about the individuals who influence her life now. While much of the vibe on *25* might be reminiscent of Adele's previous work, there is a subtle shift, and it would seem apt to break with the age labelling on her next album. However, numbers have become an important part of Adele's brand, and it may prove difficult to break with tradition now.

Adele has influenced other artists immensely, most recently Taylor Swift, whose album, *1989*, was named after the year she was born. While Swift's album title seems purposeful, with the album's retro sound mirroring the year it is named for, Adele's choice of album titles is largely incidental. When *Blues and Soul* magazine asked Adele why she named her debut album *19* she said,

"Because I couldn't come up with anything else!"[54]

Adele had a lot to say on the topic of album titles when speaking to Zane Lowe, and also said,

> I feel like the idea of calling albums after my age is showing a photograph almost of what's going on in my life then and there. I feel like not that much is going to change profoundly in me from now on in terms of how important eras of my life are to myself. So I think the next one will probably be called *Adele*. It will be, I'm not joking.[55]

While Adele's statement seems to be a little premature, especially as she is only 27, and not the much older woman she often projects through her work, it makes sense that, as an artist, Adele has explored a particular era of her work. Whatever follows will surely take her into a new place, a different territory, one which she needn't mark with an age or a year. I think Adele might be underestimating her own ability to change, and develop, however. Plus, no one can predict their own future so accurately, or know how they'll feel in a week's time, let alone a year's.

In December of 2015, *The Sun* quoted Adele as having said of *25*, "There are definitely four or five other songs that I would definitely revisit. We didn't finish it in time, and also it just felt like maybe I should be, like, 32 when I do it rather than 27?"[56] Although this sounds like a joke made in typical Adele fashion, it seems perfectly reasonable to assume that Adele's fourth album may be quite a while in the future. As a trilogy, *19* through *25* can be viewed a collection in which recurrent themes are explored, characters are revisited, and hearts are fixed only to be broken again. Perhaps Adele's next outing won't deal with the level of heartbreak her original trilogy has, instead kick-starting a fresh and unexpected era full of possibility and new sound. *32*, if we really have to wait that long, is sure to be epic.

Why is Adele's music so sad? And are all of Adele's songs really about an ex-boyfriend?

Right from the beginning, Adele has been discussing the exes and relationships which have inspired her writing. Speaking to *Blues and Soul* in 2008, Adele said,

> I still don't know exactly what kind of artist I want to be! You know, for me the album was just about making a record of songs to get a boy off my chest and include all the different kinds of music that I love.[57]

Following the release of *19*, Adele told *The Telegraph*, "Like, I wrote nine songs on the album in a three-week burst, after breaking up with my last boyfriend. I actually chucked him by text because I couldn't do it to his face. But, I haven't written any since because I've had nothing to write about."[58] She also discussed a more recent relationship in *The Telegraph*, and said,

> I started seeing this boy a couple of months ago. It was really amazing and I started trying to write songs again, and then he turned around and told me he couldn't go on with it – he couldn't handle the paparazzi, plus he was paranoid that I was going to write about him.[59]

Writing songs about ex-boyfriends is a trope most used by fellow pop star, Taylor Swift, but it seems as though Adele was always destined to be the Queen of writing sad pop ballads about ex-lovers. There is often so much overlap between the Adele and Swift, and their penchant for writing love songs about exes, that it's a surprise they've yet to work together.

Several interviews detail the inspiration behind 'Someone Like You,' and Adele's co-writer on the song, Dan Wilson, spoke to *American Songwriter* about the writing process. Wilson said,

She told me she wanted to write a song about her heartbreak... that was how she put it. She told me a little bit about the guy who broke up with her, and I think maybe part of my contribution was to keep the song really simple and direct – very personal.

It's enlightening to hear this part of the process, from her co-writer, and understand the thought that went into creating one of the most popular songs of all time. When Wilson was asked to describe what the song is about, he said,

'Someone Like You' is a love song from the point of view of a woman who shows up unexpectedly at her married ex's front door, only to be confronted by the fact that he's moved on and has a life and a wife. Whereas she's never been able to let go. The chorus is ironic: she says she's going to find someone else, but the strange and obsessive part is that she wants to find someone like him. Hopefully not to re-live the entire sad and sordid tale, but one somehow suspects that it will be so. [60]

This is such a great summation of the song by its co-writer, particularly as Wilson gives us insight into the complicated emotions running throughout

'Someone Like You'.[61] The narrator both wishes to move on, but to do so with a partner similar to the one who has left her behind. There's something messed up about this premise, the urge to start again from scratch overcome by an overwhelming nostalgia for the past. Despite acknowledging that the previous relationship didn't work out, and that there's a real need to genuinely move on for good, there's a hypnotic circling of old feelings, almost as if the real hope is that the person will come to their senses and come back. Because, after all, why write a love song directly addressing an ex unless you hope that they'll hear it and know everything you're thinking and feeling? Just sayin'.

Before a live performance of 'Someone Like You' at the Royal Albert Hall, recorded on 22 September 2011, Adele discussed her hopes for the song, and the catharsis it had given her. Adele said,

> ...I know it's a break-up record, and I'm really bitchy on it, but the guy that it's about changed my life, and we were so in love and we had so much fun – it was fucking brilliant our time together. And we are friends, because it is important that I share what is going on with this record with him... I know I play the victim on the album but... That poor boy! He's a villain these days, isn't he?![62]

Hearing Adele discuss the single with such a huge audience at her performance at the Royal Albert Hall adds another layer to the song. Not only does she reveal that she's discussed the song and its success with the ex that it's about, but that every time she performs it is a transformative experience, so that she's forever influenced by that person and their time together. Her explanation of 'Someone Like You' and its importance to her shows personal growth and development – in being able to be "friends" with her ex ("we don't hang out proper together, because that's just a bit weird, because I think you always want to end up getting back together."[63]) Adele had begun to make peace with the past. Sure, that peace feels far from complete, particularly in her description of her ex-partner at this gig – "He's very happy these days. Yeah, it's very good for him," was just one of the cutting asides she made when discussing him. But it was a beginning, and an important one. Adele could see that she owed a lot to that person and the song she wrote as a result of their relationship. When she said that that person changed her life unalterably, and continues to do so, it's a crucial truth in Adele's narrative. Sometimes we are irreparably changed by the people we meet and there's nothing we can do about it. Well, we can make a lot of money off of it, I guess, in Adele's case.

Adele spoke to *Fair Lady Magazine* in September 2011, and said, "I had to come to terms with the fact that I'd met the love of my life but it was just bad timing."[64] Adele also spoke to *Vogue* in February 2012 about the influence her love life had had on her song writing, and vice versa, and said that people should, "Be brave and fearless to know that even if you do make a wrong decision, you're making it for a good reason."[65] Adele is continually keen to share her own experiences with the world and the lessons she has learned as a result. She's an advocate of making bold choices, and knowing that sometimes the difficult decisions are the ones a person has to make. Even in times of distress, it's important to move forward, to strive for new and better.

Despite *25* being dubbed a make-up album rather than a break-up album, Adele's songs still make reference to old relationships, and the video for 'Hello' in particular appears to document the breakdown of a romance. It's as if Adele is keen to distance herself from the idea that she only writes about exes – after all, she is happily ensconced with her child's father, Simon Konecki – and wishes to show that her material has evolved. Speaking to *Sirius XFM*, Adele said,

There is some darkness on it just because I like to do dramatic, I'm a bit of a drama queen. It's not as themed as my last record. The reason I labelled it a 'make-up record,' it sounds super cliché, but my last record was labelled a 'break-up record,' and rightly so, because it was a break-up record. This record is all about how I feel as opposed to how someone else has made me feel, it's about how I made myself feel.[66]

It's enlightening to hear Adele describe herself as "a bit of a drama queen", as although she is regarded as funny and charming, and an emotional singer, it's good to know that she doesn't take herself too seriously. Quoted in *The Telegraph* in 2011, Adele said, "On record, I can get pretty dark, but in real life I'm very carefree. But when I'm happy, I ain't writing songs, I'm out having a laugh, being in love. If I ever get married, it'll be 'Darling, I need a divorce, it's been three years, I've got a record to write!'"[67] While it seems that Adele has found a way around her old issue of not being able to write when in a happy relationship, it's funny to hear her joke about the fact that she enjoys life too much to be sad all of the time. She might sound like a right misery queen on record, but Adele most definitely isn't wallowing in her spare time when she can avoid it.

Despite not writing about an ex-boyfriend anymore in the same way, Adele is still writing about ex-boyfriends, and perhaps she always will be. While it's true that Adele has diversified, and developed an emotionally varied sound, she's still addressing old relationships. However, the songs on *25* often look at past relationships from a different viewpoint. Instead of assigning blame, or discussing past hurts, Adele's new material feels more retrospective and purposeful. She's examining her own role in previous relationships, and wondering how much she's changed since. Instead of singing about how she'll never find someone else, Adele's lyrics talk about what's happened in the interim years and what she learned from those experiences. It's a more mature lyricist speaking, a person who knows there's always a chance to start over. For instance, in new song 'When We Were Young', the narrator bumps into an old flame and reminisces about the time they spent together. Instead of being melancholic, the song has a melodic quality. There's a real admiration for the person in question: Adele describes the old flame as lovely to see and hear, and reminiscent of their younger days.[68] Where 'Someone Like You' is injected with a sadness throughout, documenting loss, 'When We Were Young' looks back on a relationship after more time has passed, from a vantage point at which the positives can be seen, finally.

However, Adele has definitely not moved away from her comfort zone, despite claims to the contrary. If, for instance, Adele had released her version of Sia's single 'Alive' which was, at one point, the plan, then it could be claimed she was developing a whole new upbeat sound, and that her lyrics reflected as much.[69] Instead, 'Alive' ended up on Sia's latest album *This Is Acting*. Adele seems very comfortable in the remit of writing about exes, and deviating from this subject matter doesn't appear to come easily to her. Sure, some of her new material takes into account her changed life, with long-term partner and child. Like on 'Water Under The Bridge' when Adele is confident the relationship she's in is good and muses on its longevity.[70] But on other tracks, there's less of a departure, and we find Adele still reflecting on the past, perpetually trapped by her unhappy experiences, as on 'Million Years Ago' when she sings that she must have known the inevitability of her circumstances.[71] Adele may have evolved, but there is still a grand sense of foreboding throughout *25*.

Speaking in *The Guardian*, Adele described new song 'Send My Love (To Your New Lover)', and said, "This is my fuck-you song." Journalist Tom Lamont writes, "It was written in reference to the last guy, that never-named ex who dumped her when she was young, inspiring the best and saddest songs on *21*."[72] Designating it a "fuck-you song" rather than misery anthem elevates Adele's material to a new level, but has she really moved on? She claims she has, particularly in *The Guardian* when she said, "It sounds obvious, but I think you only learn to love again when you fall in love again. I'm in that place. My love is deep and true with my man, and that puts me in a position where I can finally reach out a hand to the ex. Let him know I'm over it."[73] Call me crazy, but a "fuck-you song" doesn't seem very much like an "I'm over it" song. Thematically, it's the same subject matter, swirling around a brain all these years later, finding other forms to mould itself into, Play-Doh-style. A song that's truly about moving on, being completely over a person or an event that's troubled us for the longest time, would surely take on another form entirely, like Alanis Morissette's 'This Grudge' which addresses the fact that for she has held her grudge for nearly a decade and a half.[74] Morissette doesn't just address the fact that her grudge against this individual has more than run its course, in taking her time and her life, she also notes the amount her feelings about this person have influenced her career: the subject appears in songs and diaries, and has been reviled in public enough to earn a bit of credit for her work.[75] Morissette's song is an example of being over something; Adele's music is still lingering in unrequited love territory, forever wondering at that ex and where they are right now.

I don't for a second blame Adele for rehashing old territory – hell, I'm still writing about every one of my own exes. And as an artist, Adele doesn't recycle her exes to quite the same degree as some other artists, like Taylor Swift, for instance. Swift famously includes clues in the liner notes of her albums[76], which hint at who particular songs are about (seriously, she does). Adele's famously secretive about her exes and refuses to comment on specifics even years later, and that's admirable for a person as famous as she is. Adele is respectful of her previous love interests, at least in some respects, and isn't using them specifically to sell albums. She can keep a secret, even if she wears her own heart on her sleeve.

Yet tabloids have long speculated over who Adele's songs are about. In an article titled 'Rolling With The Creep', *The New York Post* named "Slinky Sunbeam" who "hails from the seaside town of Margate"[77] as the inspiration behind Adele's music. While he certainly sounds like a charmer, other magazines had other theories. *Heat Magazine* claimed that a photographer called "Alex Sturrock" was in fact the much-written-about ex, with a source allegedly telling them, "He's a very normal guy and they'd laugh a lot together, eat junk food and ignore the fact that her career was about to go stratospheric."[78] While any romance that's really true love involves eating junk food together, the source told *Heat*, "It was such a volatile relationship and very passionate. When things ended between them there was a lot of animosity and anger."[79] Whether either of these claims is true is anyone's guess, but the fact remains that Adele has kept tight-lipped on the identity of the ex mentioned in her songs, and there's an element of respect at play in her public persona regarding this matter. Though the fact that she's not intent on letting the subject lie is a point to bear in mind.

In interviews Adele has always been keen to distance herself from celebrities who also write about exes. It's a deflection technique to keep the identities of the men in her life a secret, but in doing so, she often slanders other singers. In an interview with *The Guardian*, when asked who her songs were about, Adele said, "Who cares? Nobody famous, just old boyfriends. I don't date celebrities. I ain't fucking Taylor Swift, dyouknowhatImean?"[80] In hindsight, this was likely a misguided thing to say. After all, Swift is one of Adele's contemporaries, the person with whom she is most often vying for awards, or sales, or views on YouTube. And really, how different is it? Both singers write about men that they've dated. Sure, Swift's love interests are generally much more famous than Adele's, but the *1989* singer keeps as tight-lipped as Adele does about the actual identity of the people her songs are inspired by. Adele's earlier interviews are often filled with an undercurrent of snide remarks, distancing herself from her peers, and the life choices they have made (as I'll discuss later, Adele has casually thin-shamed other celebrities, including Nicole Richie).

In an interview with *TIME*, Adele said of the subject matter of her albums, "Even though my music is melancholy, there's also joy in that. I hope I do bring joy to people's lives, and not just sadness, but I think there's a comfort in it."[81] And surely that has to be part of the explanation for

Adele's immense success. Listeners connect to her work because of the range of emotions she squeezes into her songs. Sure, melancholy appears to be her default position, but there are moments of joy and happiness alongside the immense sadness that permeates her albums. It's somewhat cathartic to listen to a singer who isn't afraid to dwell on the painful moments of her life, the ones on which we spent too much time obsessing, trying to understand the people who have hurt us the most. Everyone has likely had a moment of "What if?" and Adele's had many. In the way that "Misery Memoirs" were once so popular, Adele's success appears to stem from her ability to tap into the human subconscious, and to detail the obsessive thoughts that spring from break-ups, cheating, and relationship-induced misery. We need Adele because we can't be happy all the time, can we? Plus, everyone's been dumped at least once, right?

PART 2
'HELLO'

So, 'Hello' broke a lot of records?

Since the public first heard a snippet of 'Hello',
it's been ever-present in the public consciousness.
Fans took to Twitter when a snippet of the single
was previewed during an ad break of *The X Factor*
on 18 October 2015. *The Guardian* wrote, "The
30-second clip featured no faces, names or dates,
just a black screen, some simple piano chords and
Adele's recognisable voice singing the following
lines, as the lyrics flashed up."[82] It was a simple
moment, and while it didn't even mention Adele at
all, it had viewers hooked. Social media was rife
with discussion about the snippet and what it could
mean. It was a smart piece of marketing which got
the public talking about Adele again instantly, and
it's really no wonder that the song has since gone
on to break many records.

In its first 24 hours on YouTube, the official
music video for 'Hello' clocked up over 27.7 million
views, rising to 100 million views in just five days.
Vocativ created a tally[83], pitting Adele against other
artists whose videos had reached over 100 million

views, which 'Hello' will have done in only 88 days. For comparison, the nearest competitor, Psy's 'Gangnam Style' took 159 days to achieve the same feat.

The official YouTube blog congratulated Adele on her 'Hello' success and said, "Within 48 hours, it had been viewed 50 million times, making it the biggest debut of any video on YouTube in 2015 and one of the most-watched music video debuts of all time."[84] The success of 'Hello' is unanimous, continuous, and worldwide. Adele's first single from her third album has surpassed all expectation, and is sure to continue breaking records and winning awards throughout 2016.

What is going on in the music video?

As the video for 'Hello' was watched over 3.3 million times within its first week of release,[85] you've likely seen it. If you've somehow managed to escape the pure heaven/torture that is the most watched music video of all time, I'm impressed. But there's one thing you need to know about 'Hello' – it's a smorgasbord of music video cliché.

Shot in black and white, the video is back-to-back cliché. Whether or not the clichés are intentional is anyone's guess, though it's difficult to imagine including most of the video's motifs without considering that perhaps they're well-worn riffs already. For instance, the lingering shots of British phone boxes feel ham-fisted at best, as if the director was playing a word association game and it was the best idea anyone came up with. Aside from cliché, the music video for 'Hello' is mostly interested in showcasing the fact that Adele is ready for her own make-up campaign right now, with close-ups of her precise eyeliner, and coifed hair being the focal point of most shots.

The 'Hello' video opens with an image of a dirty window, which might not sound like much, but wait, it gets better. The shot comes into focus, revealing a road winding towards the building the camera's in, and a car driving along it. And in the next shot, we see Adele, albeit through dirty glass, speaking on her mobile phone. She says that she's losing her signal and apologises.[86] Then Adele closes her flip-phone with a certain degree of frustration and finality, though the shot's more about her perfectly manicured fingernails that would give any Kardashian a run for their money. Further evidence that Adele's pitching for her own cosmetics line or endorsement finally? Just sayin'.

Adele walks into the house, door creaking like it's in a horror film, and she stands in the hallway, her impressive outfit reminding us that she's a big star now. She whips a white sheet from a decrepit window, covering herself in dust, and symbolically pulls blankets and covers from chairs, undressing this abandoned building, trying to bring it to life. The sheer quantity of dust in the air in this video, through aesthetically sumptuous, is asthma-inducing. All of this takes place even before the music starts.

One of the most important moments of the video is a tight shot of Adele's face. Her eyes are closed, and her head lolls about for the camera, catching the light just so, yet still managing to suggest a full neck spin is possible, akin to *The Exorcist*. The music starts playing when Adele's eyes open. It's an unsubtle visual cue: Adele is back from hibernation, alert like an alarm clock's buzzing next to her face and she can feel the vibrations. Of course, the shot cuts away before Adele can open her mouth and mime the words to 'Hello', but the eye-opening is the sort of high-impact trope you'd expect from an artist that loves melodrama this much.

Adele's visually absent through the first lines of 'Hello'. Instead, a stove is lit, an old-fashioned kettle is placed on top, and a cup of tea is made. I can only assume that this is supposed to geographically place us in England, or remind us that Adele's British in case we forgot in the years since *21*. And the next time we see Adele again, she's sipping said tea, from a vintage china tea cup, no less. If it wasn't before, her brand is now chintz.

Once the tea's made, we get our first shot of the love interest, although I'm sure you've not forgotten that 'Hello' isn't about a relationship. You'll be forgiven if the video suggests to you that it is. Shot like home video footage, Adele's beau is shot almost completely in slow motion (slow-mo, after all, is the epitome of cliché), and each time we see him he's in conversation with the camera, or Adele, or us. His presence is meant to function like memory – a snapshot of a moment, replaying years later. As the video progresses, so does the relationship, degenerating from domesticated moments of fun during which he attempts to feed her directly from a pan, to full-on arguments and, worst of all, him walking away in the rain, in slow motion of course.

The second verse begins with a measured shot of a telephone box. Despite being filmed in Canada, the phone box is one of those old-school British red ones (I mean, I presume it's red – the black-and-white stifles the colour of it). Overgrown and, for some unknown reason, in the middle of a forest, the phone has fallen from the receiver. Derelict, and completely misplaced, the box is yet another tired analogy for the past. Telephone boxes of this variety are museum pieces at this point, and including a relic from the UK's history grounds the video in an alternate time. We get it. All the telephones are old, and none of them can reach the people they need to. Some lines are cut, and some calls can't be made despite any number of redials. Adele can't reach the past any more than the rest of us can.

The rest of the video rolls out just as you'd expect. There are multiple shots of the love interest in the rain, shouting at the camera. Adele looks from an upstairs window, peeking from behind netting, as the love interest loads the trunk of his car, hangs up his flip phone (what is it with all these flip phones?), and drives away. The repeated motif of him walking away in the rain, in slow-mo, feels a little overwrought, but is surely meant to evidence the fact that the moments we remember aren't always the perfect ones; sometimes it's the worst moments that stick in our brains like lesions.

Perhaps the most dramatic shot of the video is when Adele stands on the smallest island, surrounded by water, as a wind machine blows her hair and her outfit all out of shape. It's dramatic, filmic, and acts as an audition for Adele's future Las Vegas residency. If she can handle a wind machine, she can handle anything, right?

While the video doesn't break much new ground, *per se*, for Adele or the form of the music video, the fact that it has been parodied quite so much is surely a sign of its universality. Particularly, its use of iconic props and imagery – overgrown British telephone boxes, flip phones, metal kettles, and slow-mo – have made 'Hello' ripe for the picking when it comes to comedy. Everyone, from James Corden to Matthew McConaughey on *Saturday Night Live* to The Muppets, has made a version of the video, and I doubt we've seen the last take off. Most recently, Adele took part in Carpool Karaoke, a segment on James Corden's *The Late Late Show in the US*, and the preview for her appearance opened with Corden uttering the lyrics to 'Hello' while he waited for Adele in the car. He hammed it up for the camera, somewhat unsubtly.[87]

If anything, Adele's 'Hello' video has made her synonymous with the flip phone, something we all thought long-dead. Though perhaps long-dead is exactly what Adele is going for? After all, her relationship analysis is akin to picking over the turkey carcass weeks after Christmas hoping to find an explanation for the bird's demise. Despite the PR machine surrounding the release of 'Hello', the video is absolutely about a break-up, re-hashing a relationship for answers to age old questions. The excruciating detail with which the video performs this autopsy is responsible for the worldwide hysteria the song has created – Adele discusses things we're all thinking, about relationships, break-ups, tiny moments in which we wished we'd acted differently, but didn't. The fact that the video is in black and white is the icing on a diabetes-inducing cake; it represents the past, and none of us can get back to it, however hard we try. Apart from Adele of course, *because* she's Adele, and she can visit her past at a moment's notice, just to witness the love of her life walking away from her in slow motion in the rain, like a rom-com you saw but likely forgot about because it was a bit shit.

Who is the hot guy playing her ex? Wasn't he in *90210*?

The man playing the object of Adele's affection in the 'Hello' music video is Tristan Wilds, an American actor and singer-songwriter. Wilds is best known for his roles in HBO's *The Wire*, and *90210*, the reboot of the classic '90s show. His debut album, *New York: A Love Story*, received a Grammy nomination in 2014 in the Best Urban Contemporary Album category.

Speaking to *Entertainment Weekly* the week 'Hello' was released, Tristan Wilds detailed the way that the video's director, Xavier Dolan, initially contacted him on Skype. Wilds said,

> It was dope. So as soon as he reached out, I was excited and I wanted to see what he had to talk about and what his thought process was behind it. And once we got on the Skype and he started speaking about it, just his passion behind it and how much he wanted to put into it and the emotions that he wanted to get across sold me. I told him, 'If you want me, you got me. I'm completely 100 percent in it.'[88]

Which seems a smart move considering the level of attention 'Hello' has garnered, particularly in breaking so many records. If Tristan Wilds was recognised selectively prior to 'Hello', now he's famous worldwide, cast in the all-important role of Adele's ex.

Tristan Wilds described the making of the video for 'Hello' as a very collaborative process. He told *Entertainment Weekly*, "A lot of stuff that we did it was Xavier's brainchild, so a lot of what we did was very much so improvisation.

He kind of asked both of us to tap into our own past relationships and feelings and situations."[89] This way of working is undoubtedly grounded in Xavier Dolan's process as a director, but it's still interesting to note that the video's focus is very much on a past relationship. In asking Wilds and Adele to channel past relationships and break-ups during filming suggests that the video's interpretation of 'Hello' is that it's a break-up song. Even though Adele keeps insisting it's not. Okay.

Wilds spoke at length with *Entertainment Weekly* about working with Adele, and was completely complimentary about the process. He said, "Usually people are very awestruck, and at first I was – she's a very, very beautiful young lady – but I think very, very quickly in, she made it easy for everyone to feel at home."[90] The chemistry between Wilds and Adele certainly seems very real, despite them only featuring in the same shot once – the iconic moment that Adele's hands reach out and hold Wilds's face. Otherwise, the two are kept very separate, which hints at the fact that two people experience the same relationship differently, and that once committed to memory and firmly placed in the past, a person becomes packaged up like a relic, no longer a human being we can interact with.

Perhaps the most pertinent moment in

Wilds's interview with *Entertainment Weekly*, aside from the discussion which ensued about Adele's acting aspiration (something we must return to later), was when *EW* asked Wilds if he could "feel when you were making it that this was something special, that this was going to be big?" Wilds's response is fairly Hollywood-typical, and borderline cliché: "It's crazy, I think the ones that are usually the most successful, the parts or the shows or anything that are the most successful or the most iconic, you don't necessarily always feel it... It was just fun. There wasn't pressure. It was legit us there just having a great time."[91]

Having had some time to reflect on the success of 'Hello', Wilds gave a follow-up interview to *ABC News* in December 2015, in which he discussed how hugely successful the single had been. Talking about the director of 'Hello', Xavier Dolan, Wilds said, "He kept telling me he doesn't want to do a regular music video. He didn't even want it to be considered a music video. He wanted to shoot a film."[92] The 'Hello' video is certainly cinematic in appearance. In featuring improvisations by both Adele and Tristan Wilds, an underlying plot is developed. Sure, it's not unusual for a music video to feature a recognisable or even famous actor, or to be aesthetically pleasing.

But Dolan's aspirations are clear, particularly as several of the scenes are filmed in IMAX.[93] 'Hello' is a piece of art as much as it's a common or garden music video.

Speaking to *ABC News*, Wilds reiterated the emotions involved in his performance, as he explained that his character was "someone going through heartbreak. It's love lost. That's easy to pull from. That's an emotion that we all go through."[94] Love lost, but definitely not about an ex-boyfriend. Got it. Wilds's own feelings about Adele are clear: "I was just in awe in how giving she was. She's genuine and just a really cool girl. She's real chill."[95]

Some of the most interesting critique of 'Hello' and Tristan Wilds's performance has come from a feminist standpoint. Leia Smoudianis, of *The Feminism Project*, wrote,

> It's still a rarity to see interracial couples in movies, TV, ads, or music videos... And trust me, I notice these things! Being in an interracial relationship (the boyfriend is Chinese-Canadian) I always look for couples in the media that represent my situation. Unfortunately, there are few options, and when I find them they usually disappoint. Like *The Walking Dead*'s on-screen example of Maggie and Glenn –

does it have to be the end of the world for a white woman to marry an Asian man? So good for Adele for including some diversity in her videos!"[96]

Smoudianis's point is an important one, one which television show runner Shonda Rhimes continues to pioneer when she says, "I feel like the television landscape should look like the world we see outside".[97] Shannon Carling, of *Medium*, concurred that it was "a bold casting choice to feature an African American actor as Adele's ex-lover without making it the whole point of the video."[98] In fact, Carling went so far as to say that the video for 'Hello' is progress, as "race is not part of the plot in any way. It's just colourblind casting in the most positive sense of the word."[99] Not everyone agreed, however, with FAF Magazine compiling negative Twitter reactions to the video under the headline 'Adele's New Music Video 'Hello' Has An Interracial Couple And Some People Can't Deal'.[100]

'Hello' has definitely put Tristan Wilds back on the map, and given him an international audience and incredible viewership. As Wilds himself said, "You get me, Xavier and Adele in a room and magic's going to happen. We did amazing work so the work speaks for itself."[101] The world seems to agree.

PART 3

What's the story behind the record?

Adele's been quite vocal about writing and recording *25*. In a post on Twitter, Adele wrote, drop caps hers,

> this feels like such a long time coming, my new album is finally out. i am so overwhelmed and grateful to be able to even put another record out, and put it out how i want. the last month has been a whirlwind, its literally taken my breath away. i hope you enjoy the record as much as i enjoyed making it for you. see you on the other side... love adele x.[102]

In interviews, Adele has discussed the fact that *25* took a long time to get right. Writing for *Rolling Stone*, Brian Hiatt said,

> About a year and a half ago, Adele thought she might have nearly enough songs for an album. Her manager wasn't so sure, and they brought the demos to Rick Rubin, who had given valuable input on *21*... He looked at Adele and told her, 'I don't believe you.'

The original group of songs was lighter in tone than anything she's done.[103]

Describing that original version of *25* to Hiatt, Adele said, "You know the pop songs that are fantastic, but they don't have much depth? They were all a bit like that."[104] It would've been all too easy for Adele to release that version of *25*, and it's a real testament to her authenticity as an artist that she scrapped many of those tracks. It also shows Adele to be quite a perfectionist, not happy to settle on a product if there's the slightest doubt or her heart's not in it.

Adele worked with several co-writers while recording *25*, and one of those was fellow pop star Sia. As well as being a successful solo artist (Sia refuses to be photographed or filmed, so wears a wig to all public appearances, which covers most of her face), Sia has written hit songs for some of the biggest pop stars in the world. She's responsible for Rihanna's 'Diamonds', Beyoncé's 'Pretty Hurts', and has collaborated with artists like Lea Michele, Kanye West, Eminem, and Kylie Minogue. Speaking to *Billboard*, Sia's producer Jesse Shatkin said,

> I did a few days with Adele and Sia in the studio... and that was mind-blowing just to be there, to hang out with her and witness two great minds working together. I had

been working on some other songs for her record possibly, so I had devoted a few weeks of my life to getting in the zone for doing stuff for Adele. I was thrilled about it the whole time.[105]

The mere idea of Adele's working with Sia is pretty spectacular on paper, although, as it turned out, the collaboration didn't make it on to *25*. Speaking to *Billboard*, Shatkin said, "We heard very soon that she didn't think it was right for her. Then we thought about sending it to Rihanna, and then once Sia put her vocal on it, she was like, 'I can't let this go. I need it for me.' Her label and management agreed."[106] It's so interesting to get an insight like this into Adele's writing process, particularly as her songs always feel so personal, pared down, and emotionally raw. Knowing that Adele spent some time writing with such a successful songwriter as Sia is surprising, and perhaps evidence that Adele was keen to try new things with this record, and in studio sessions was working on a more generic pop sound. That their collaboration didn't create anything suitable for Adele's new album is a shame, but Sia wasn't the only writing partner whose work didn't get used. Of the time she spent in the studio with Blur frontman Damon Albarn, Adele told *Rolling Stone*, "It ended up being one of those 'don't meet your idol' moments. The saddest thing was that I was such a big Blur fan growing up. But it was sad, and I regret hanging out with him."[107] Burn.

In a post on Twitter on 21 October 2015, Adele said,

> Turning 25 was a turning point for me, slap bang in the middle of my twenties. Teetering on the edge of being an old adolescent and a fully-fledged adult, I made the decision to go into becoming who I'm going to be forever without a removal full of my old junk... 25 is about getting to know who I've become without realising. And I'm sorry it took so long, but you know, life happened.[108]

Notably, Adele turned 27 before *25* was released, but her incessant desire to document years in her life, and events that have taken place in the interim, functions as a "Dear Diary" of sorts. Although not all of the songs appear to be autobiographical, it seems as though Adele is keen to bookmark the important stages in her life. As such, *25* heralds in a new era, particularly as on Twitter Adele also said, "My last record was a break-up record and if I had to label this one I would call it a make-up record. I'm making up with myself. Making up for lost time." While 'Hello' certainly sounds like a "break-up record,"[109] it's worth noting that Adele views this period of her career as being about reparation, and taking stock of events that have come to pass. While it reflects on relationships in much the same way as her previous work, 25 stands apart in its change of perspective. The narrator, looking back, has come to terms with some of her losses, and can actually see strengths in what were previously considered to be negatives. Adele has most definitely evolved, and her music with her.

Why can't I stream 25?

Following the release of 'Hello', Adele fans had one big question: would new album 25 be on Spotify on its release date, 20 November 2015? In an interview with TIME, published in December 2015, Adele discussed her decision to not allow 25 to be streamed. Adele said, "I believe music should be an event. For me, all albums that come out, I'm excited about leading up to release day. I don't use streaming. I buy my music. I download it, and I buy a physical just to make up for the fact that someone else somewhere isn't. It's a bit disposable, streaming."[110] This follows Taylor Swift's decision to remove her music from Spotify and not allow recent album *1989* to be streamed.[111] While Adele's argument is certainly interesting, clinging to an antiquated idea of what an album should be, it feels more like a smart business decision. A business decision that most definitely paid off, considering the sales of *25* to date. The same can be said of Swift's move with album *1989*. In both cases, it can be argued that the albums may not have sold in quite the astronomical numbers they did in their respective first weeks had they been available to stream.

Still, I'm fascinated by Adele's insistence that *25* not be available on streaming services is purely a matter of taste and, in her case, a desire for listeners to mirror her music habits. Speaking to *TIME* in December 2015, Adele also said, "I know that streaming music is the future, but it's not the only way to consume music. I can't pledge allegiance to something that I don't know how I feel about yet."[112] While Adele admitted that streaming was undoubtedly the way the music industry was heading, she was yet unconvinced by it, and as such refused to commit to it. However, by making this choice, Adele is limiting fan access to her music. While Adele may feel that enjoying an album is about having a physical product or downloading a complete album, she's excluding those who cannot afford to purchase the album outright, and rely on the likes of Spotify to access music. I'm sure this is not a concern of Adele's, though, and not allowing *25* on streaming services has clearly been a great financial move: at least some of the album sales must be down to more people having to purchase it, rather than being able to experience it elsewhere. Adele is definitely an astute business woman, whose old-school values when it comes to music-purchasing may be as much about financial acumen as they are about retaining authenticity.

Curiously, Adele's previous albums, *19* (2008) and *21* (2011),[113] are both currently available on Spotify, as is single 'Hello', perhaps evidence that Adele is not as vehemently opposed to streaming as she claims. Clever marketing ploy, anyone?

PART 4
WORLD DOMINATION

Tell me about Adele's *25* world tour.

Following the humungous success of Adele's single 'Hello', and subsequent album release, news started circulating that a World Tour to accompany her new music was imminent. Adele didn't make fans wait too long before confirming her plans on 26 November 2015. Via her Facebook page, the singer shared an exclusive video clip in which she said, "I have been bluffing this whole time and I'm so relieved to finally tell you that I am of course coming on tour, and I can't wait to see all of you there."[114] Adele announced the news in a series of disastrous (somewhat staged) antics, even uttering the words, 'Hello, it's me!' before bursting out laughing. Standing in front of a map of Europe, like a weather person or a warlord intent on domination, Adele proved once again that despite her dulcet tones, she is very much here to conquer.

Adele initially confirmed 34 European tour dates, beginning on 29 February 2016 in Ireland, and ending in Belgium in mid-June. This number later grew to 49 European shows following the incredible demand. Tickets went on sale 4 December 2015 and, as widely expected, sold out quickly. Despite implementing a special ticketing service though website Songkick, designed to identify touts attempting to buy tickets, many fans found themselves unsuccessful in their quest to purchase any.[115] According to *The Independent*, "Adele rescued 36,000 tickets from the hands of touts by controlling sales for her 2016 tour through her own website... more than 18,000 'known or likely touts' were de-registered before the UK pre-sale tickets were made available."[116] It appears as though Adele was adamant that tickets for her tour went to real fans wherever possible, and didn't fall into the hands of touts who would attempt to sell them on for exorbitant prices. Of course, it's impossible to control event tickets completely, and it's likely that some people will end up paying over the odds to gain access to one of Adele's concerts. Still, it's a testament to the singer-songwriter that she was keen to try and give fans as fair a chance as any to see her live.

Adele made the United States wait a little longer before she announced the remaining dates in her World Tour. On 14 December 2015, Adele posted a link on Twitter[117] to a page on her website, where she officially listed the 2016

North American tour dates, of which there are 56 shows.[118] Adrienne Green writes for *The Atlantic*, "Tickets went on sale Thursday morning, but unfortunately for the thousands of people who were repeatedly refreshing their browsers, tickets sold out within minutes on Stubhub, there were longer-than-usual wait times on Ticketmaster, and the singer's website blocked many purchases."[119] Whilst it was widely predicted that tickets for Adele's tour would sell out incredibly quickly, fans were understandably peeved at missing out. For instance, *The Atlantic* cites Twitter user @ the_alyssa_noll who tweeted, "Hello from the ticket lineee. I must have tried 639947 times. To tell you, I WANT #adeletickets."[120] Better luck next time?

What's the secret to Adele's worldwide success?

It appears that a large part of Adele's international success is her accessibility. She writes about subjects everyone understands (heartbreak), and gives listeners the chance to explore their feelings in a perfectly packaged, four-minute pop song. Adele's music is not only easily digestible, it explores themes that are universal, and never appear to run out of steam. If Taylor Swift is the queen of flippantly dissecting her relationships, Adele is the queen of melancholy, of carrying out a full autopsy on a relationship until there is nothing remaining but bones.

In December 2015, *TIME* asked Adele why she thought she had such widespread appeal. Adele said,

> The fact that I'm not shy or embarrassed to be falling apart. Everyone falls apart, I think. A lot of people try to be brave and not shed a tear. Sometimes when you know someone else feels as shit as you do, or approaches things in a certain way just like you do, it makes you feel better about yourself.[121]

By exploring the darkness of life, the mistakes, misfortunes, and sad moments, Adele has found the perfect platform from which to connect with a wide audience. Also in *TIME*, Adele said, "Even though my music is melancholy, there's also joy in that. I hope I do bring joy to people's lives, and not just sadness, but I think there's a comfort in it. But I honestly don't know. If I knew, I would bottle it, and sell it to everyone else."[122] With *25*, it appears she is doing just that, particularly as the album has sold such an excessive amount of copies. It's as good as bottling tears.

Damon Albarn allegedly called Adele's new record "middle of the road",[123] following a disagreement between the two in the studio (they were meant to be writing new material together for *25*, but didn't gel). But perhaps this is not so much an insult, as an observation. Adele's new material does have a strange appeal, in that it appears to appeal to everybody. As such, being called "middle of the road" is hardly offensive, and instead of being read for its negative connotation, can be understood an alternate way. If Adele's music is "middle of the road", then it literally appeals to everybody, and which other artists can claim that particular accolade?

Why is Adele so popular in the US?

Adele spoke to *TIME* magazine in December 2015, who asked the artist how she felt about her incredible popularity in the States. Writing on *TIME*'s website, Sam Lansky said, "Most significantly, she notched the biggest first-week sales on record when she sold a jaw-dropping 3.38 million copies in the United States. But ask her how she did it and she's absolutely baffled."[124] However, this observation of Adele suggests that her success in the US was not the slightest bit premeditated, which would be a lie. Back in April of 2008, Adele discussed her plans for album 19, with *The Telegraph* writer Husband, who said, "Now she's due some serious American money."[125] It's obvious that from early on in Adele's career, a plan was in place to break America, and said plan was obviously executed so successfully that Americans have all but claimed Adele as one of their own. As Adele told *TIME* magazine, "It's a bit ridiculous. I'm not even from America."[126] The only explanation Adele can come up with is downright strange, as in *TIME* Lansky wrote, "She sets down her cup of tea, brightening. 'Maybe they think I'm related to the Queen. Americans are *obsessed* with the royal family.'"[127] Whatever the reason is, Adele is certainly popular in the US, and her fame there shows no signs of abating.

According to *CNN*, it was Adele's performance on *Saturday Night Live* that helped cement her as a star in America. For *CNN*, Lisa Respers France said, "It was her luck to land on *SNL* the night 2008 Republican vice presidential nominee Sarah Palin made an appearance... US fans were smitten."[128] According to *CNN*, no-one anticipated the success of Adele's follow-up to *19*, *21*, and as such even Adele herself was unprepared for the way in which it gathered momentum. As

Lisa Respers France said, "The sophomore slump is real, and hopes were muted for 2011's *21*. After all, Adele had won the best new artist Grammy in 2009, and such a blessing has proved to be more of a curse for other artists."[129] But it most certainly wasn't a curse for Adele, and there's been a heightened interest in her career ever since. She overcome the nervous, negative energy that preempted her second album, and emerged victorious, and better than ever.

Adele has succeeded where so many have failed. Robbie Williams famously tried to break America when he launched a solo career,[130] but despite his attempts, it didn't happen. Those artists which have been successful are one who have committed to the cause, agreeing to tour relentlessly and do press whenever required. Natasha Bedingfield, whose initial success was in the UK, ultimately moved to the US when it became apparent she may succeed there. This move included postponing a sold out UK tour twice, and then cancelling it altogether.[131] While Adele is committed to England, and it's firmly her home, her American success seems to have come easier than it does for many and this fact, in part, must be down to her song-writing ability. Regardless of location in the world, people connect with Adele's music

and lyrics in a way they don't with anyone else's.
She's an impressive Brit, that's for sure.

PART 5
IDEOLOGY

What are Adele's politics, and does it matter? And what was all that talk of her not wanting to pay tax?

While Adele has always claimed to be a staunch Labour Party supporter, she's also been incredibly outspoken regarding the amount of tax she has to pay. Speaking to *Q magazine* in May 2011, she said, "I use the NHS. I can't use public transport anymore, doing what I do. I went to state school. I'm mortified to have to pay 50%. Trains are always late, most state schools are shit and I've gotta give you, like, four million quid? Are you having a laugh?"[132] Considering that Adele went to the BRIT School, which is funded by the state, her comments are pretty shocking. While there might be an element of sarcasm at play, Adele has been quite firm about being unhappy about her tax bill. Perhaps the most concerning statement Adele made was when she said, "When I got my tax bill in from *19* I was ready to go and buy a gun and randomly open fire."[133] A totally inappropriate comment for a person of Adele's stature to make, particularly in reference to the fact that she's a multi-millionaire. It's surprising that more of her fans didn't pay greater attention to her comments on this matter, particularly her so-called joke about purchasing a gun and shooting it.

The Telegraph unsurprisingly defended Adele's stance on tax and said, "Welcome to Telegraph Blogs, Adele. Round here, we don't like Britain's 50p tax rate either. (It's a tax on success. And successful British stars like you are a very good thing for this country)."[134] Other papers were less kind, and predicted a backlash against the singer. Rob Fitzpatrick wrote for The Guardian, "Hearing Adele complain about being taxed on the great tidal wave of cash generated by her multi-million selling albums, it's hard to feel much sympathy."[135] Some fans took to Twitter on the topic, and their messages weren't kind. NY Daily News cited @nicklibertine who said, "Got my pay cheque today. Looking at the amount I take home after tax and national insurance is just depressing. Fuck you, Adele."[136] However, Adele's comments don't seem to have impacted her image in the long term, and she appears to have acquired the public's forgiveness quickly following her semi-outrageous comments.

Does Adele like being famous?

Adele is notoriously private, particularly since she gave birth. Speaking in *The Guardian* in November 2015, Adele was candid about being a celebrity, and said, "It's very easy to give in to being famous. Because it's charming. It's powerful. It draws you in. Really, it's harder work resisting it. But after a while I just refused to accept a life that was not real."[137] Convincing evidence that Adele's statement is true is the amount of time she took between *21*, and releasing new material on *25*. Several reports emphasise how important it was for Adele that she released the album she wanted to, even if that meant going back to the drawing board. Ryan Tedder, who collaborated with Adele on *25*, told *The NY Times* in November 2015, "The girl has probably thrown away easily 20 hits off of *25* that will at some point wander away, maybe into other artists' hands. With Adele, it's not about 'Can I get a hit? Can I sing that note? Can I get with the best producers?' It's about, 'What's the story?'"[138] It appears to be absolutely true that Adele is far more interested in living a normal everyday life than she is in being a celebrity, or releasing an album of pop hits, if it doesn't feel authentically her.

In response to the fact that she'd turned down collaborations and appearances, including Bob Geldof's *Band Aid 30*, Adele told *The Guardian*, "I know some people thought I was mad for taking a break. Even I can see it was a bit weird. But I'm glad it happened. I think it was the right thing. It slowed everything down."[139] Adele seems to be committed to getting the balance right between her work life and her home life.

Adele is fiercely protective of her son, Angelo, and even won a court case back in July 2014, ensuring that photos couldn't be taken of him. *The Guardian* said,

> The two-year-old son of singer Adele has been awarded a five-figure sum from a photo agency in settlement of a privacy case brought by his parents over paparazzi photos of his 'milestone moments'. Lawyers for Adele... said she was emphatic that Angelo Adkins was not and must never be 'public property'.[140]

Adele is by no means the only celebrity to insist on privacy for her children. Instead, she joins a whole host of famous people who have stipulated that the paparazzi must never take photos of their kids. It's a stealth example of a celebrity separating private life from public persona, something which

Adele seems to really advocate. In standing up for the rights of her child, Adele's asserting her family's privacy, and that's an important move for someone as famous as she is, catapulted into the spotlight as rapidly as she was.

While there must be some aspects of fame Adele is *au fait* with, for the most part she comes across as a hugely private person, so the fact that many of her songs are autobiographical makes her a wild contradiction. Much like her peer Lily Allen, Adele would likely be content away from the public eye. But as is the nature of the music industry, the image of a singer is often as important as their music. While Adele has proven people wrong in showing that a person doesn't have to fit a particular mould in order to be a pop star, she is still more in the public eye than, say, Sia, who never shows her face in public. Adele has made her peace with the aspects of fame that are a necessity for her career to continue, although she doesn't always seem to enjoy them much. I get the impression that she loves making music, that it's what she lives for, but she'd probably be just as happy doing that on her own, at home, away from the world. But that doesn't pay the bills, does it?

Writing for *Fortune*, Chris Morris said, "Don't however, expect Adele to radically change her philosophy toward fame. Beyond her big voice and the universal themes of her song, she achieved notoriety by not playing by the typical rules."[141] And it would appear that Adele's insistence on not playing by the music-industry mandated set of rules has served her well so far and helped make her the world-famous star she is today. Somewhat ironic considering Adele is so outspoken about not enjoying fame. Still, as she's gotten older, Adele looks more comfortable in her own skin, and seems more at ease with the lifestyle she has inherited. The fact is that Adele is a person who lives by her own rules; by dictating who can and cannot take photos of her child, or speak about her family, Adele is carving out a path all her own. And why shouldn't she, as one of the most famous people in the world? Adele has proven that being famous doesn't always automatically mean that the public has or should have unlimited access to a person's life. For Adele, privacy is important, and she'll never stop striving to retain the slither of life that is just her own.

Is Adele a feminist?

The question that every famous woman gets asked regularly is, "Are you a feminist?" While answers to the feminism question from female pop stars generally range from the disappointing to the bizarre, Adele has been consistently bold about this topic. Not only is it important for a woman of Adele's stature and popularity to align herself with feminism at a time when many are denying any connection to it, it's refreshing for a person as famous as Adele is to not shy away from questions which attempt to pigeonhole the politics of a person.

In an interview with *Rolling Stone* in November 2015, writer Brian Hiatt discussed feminism with Adele. Hiatt said,

> Adele has been so busy the past few years that she's only faintly aware of the newfound prominence of feminism in the pop-cultural discourse. 'If there's a movement, that's great,' she says. 'Who's doing it? Will you ask me if I'm a feminist? I don't think many men in interviews get asked if they're feminist.'[142]

And Adele's point is an important one. Women in the public eye are regularly asked whether or not they're feminists, when they're not being asked what brand their eye shadow is, while men are rarely questioned with either of these topics. That Adele calls out the fact that men are not religiously asked this repetitive question shows that she's not afraid of being politically pigeonholed.

Also in *Rolling Stone*, writing about Adele, Hiatt said,

> I don't ask the question, but she wants to answer anyway. 'I'm a feminist,' she says, sipping wine. 'I believe that everyone should be treated the same, including race and sexuality.' She recalls not being taken seriously in business meetings full of men, of encountering an attitude of 'what do you know?'[143]

That Adele has experienced sexism in the music industry is of little surprise, but the fact that she has confronted it head on, in an outspoken way, as you'd expect of an artist as bold as she is, speaks to her credibility.

As well as proclaiming herself a feminist, Adele continues to be outspoken about body image and what it means to be a woman in today's world. Speaking to Jenny Eliscu in a SiriusXM Town Hall, Adele said, "I do have body image problems, but I don't let them rule my life, at all. And there's bigger issues going on in the world than how I might feel about myself and stuff like that."[144] This is such a refreshing viewpoint to hear from a person as famous as Adele is. Unlike other celebrities, Adele isn't afraid of showing weakness, and it's her honesty that's attracted so many fans. Appearing to be so down to earth, and struggling with the same issues as everyone, Adele has endeared herself to the world. Exposing herself in this way, in admitting that she has the same fears, self-doubts, and body image concerns as other people, is a bold feminist move. Adele is helping to redefine what it means to be a woman in the modern world.

Does Adele have any super fans?

Adele fans are referred to by several terms. *Billboard* called fans "Adeleholics",[145] while earlier accounts claim that Adele fans are known as "Daydreamers"[146] named after a song from her album *19*, with even the official Adele website calling fans that, though this seems to have died out now.

In October 2015, *USA TODAY* published an article titled, 'Hello, Adele, it's your fans and they've lost it over your new single'.[147] In November 2015, *The New York Times* followed this up with an article titled, 'Adele Goes Viral, No Selfies Or Tweets Needed'.[148] As well as discussing the instant success of 'Hello' without any push for marketing, *The New York Times* also talked about what Adele's fan base is like. Ben Sisario said,

> Adele's success may also be because
> of her following among a demographic
> group that the youth-obsessed pop
> music world does not often focus on.
> According to Nielsen, which has studied
> the demographics of the fans of various
> pop acts, the typical Adele fan is a college-
> educated woman aged 25 to 44, who
> watches 'Family Guy' on TV and likes to
> shop at Target, Victoria's Secret and Bath &
> Body Works.[149]

It's great to see analysis this specific about Adele's
fans, and that the range of fans is fairly broad.
According to the article, the typical Adele fan is
female, and this idea that the group in question is a
demographic "that the youth-obsessed pop music
world does not often focus on,"[150] shows that as
an artist she's tapped into potential fans in need
of music they can connect to. Adele isn't afraid to
break the mould when it comes to her music, or
isn't bothered if she appears to be the remotest bit
uncool, and this is clearly approved of by her fans.

The New York Times also noted the
seriousness of Adele fans, when Sisario said,
"Adele appears to have activated millions of
customers for whom making a purchase is viewed

as a sign of devotion and support for the artist they love."[151] Adele fans are committed to products she puts out, and are keen to show their support for the artist, and interest in her, by putting their money down. Regardless of the fact that she is a multi-millionaire, Adele has inspired a level of fandom in "Adeleholics" unheard of in the internet age. She's managed to convince hoards of people to part with their money and buy a CD, an antiquated product that is surely on the brink of dying out? But if Adele's selling, fans are buying by the truckload.

PART 6
IMAGE

Adele's said a lot of positive things about body image.

As discussed in relation to Adele's feminist standpoint, Adele has undoubtedly been an important advocate for the body positivity movement. Despite being continually criticised by celebrities like Karl Lagerfeld and Joan Rivers, Adele has ignored her haters. For instance, when speaking to Jenny Eliscu, Adele said, "There's only one of you, so why would you want to look like everyone else? Why would you want to have the same hair style as everyone else and have the same opinions as everyone else?"[152] Advocating this sort of self-belief makes Adele one of the most outspoken female role models of recent times. Encouraging her fans to be themselves, and to not feel as though they have to dress the same as everyone else, is an important part of Adele's persona.

Some of the criticism against Adele and her appearance has been public and scathing. In an interview with David Letterman, Joan Rivers renamed a popular Adele single as 'Rolling in the Deep Fried Chicken'.[153] While this might seem like standard fare, the fat-shaming wasn't limited to one performance, with Rivers telling *Huffington Post*'s Marc Lamont Hill, "She's a chubby lady who's very, very rich... Adele is beautiful and successful. Let's face reality: she's fat!"[154] While Rivers managed to acknowledge the fact that Adele is an incredibly successful woman, her fat-shaming was constant. Similarly, fashion designer Karl Lagerfeld, who is renowned for commenting on women's weight publicly, famously called Adele "a little too fat".[155] In the October 2011 issue of *Vogue*, Adele responded to Lagerfeld's comments. Adele said,

> I enjoy being me; I always have done. I've seen people where it rules their lives, you know, who want to be thinner or have bigger boobs, and it wears them down. And I don't want that in my life. It's never been an issue – at least, I've never hung out with the sort of horrible people who would make it an issue. I have insecurities, of course, but I don›t hang out with anyone who points them out to me.[156]

Adele's rebuttal is, as usual, on point and brazenly honest. As a woman and an artist, Adele clearly doesn't have time for shallow criticisms, which attempt to play on existing insecurities she has. In fact, in responding to fat-shaming criticism, Adele comes out on top, aligning herself with the general public more than ever. Perhaps the most important phrase of Adele's response is, "I enjoy being me; I always have done." It shouldn't be revolutionary that a person actually likes themselves, but somehow it is. As Adele is so obviously comfortable in her own skin, she inspires a confidence and belief in her fans too.

Adele's many famous fans are quick to praise the singer's attitude to body image. In an interview with *Stylist* magazine, Lady Gaga said,

> My mum called me and was like, 'Did you gain weight?' Everybody was telling me about it, and I didn't really care. But when I heard it was on the news, where they talk about wars, the economy crashing and the election – I just thought, 'This is fucking ridiculous.' I mean, what kind of example is that to a young girl sitting at home? I thought, well I don't really care if they think I'm fat, because, quite honestly, I did gain about 30 pounds. Adele is bigger than me, how come nobody says anything about it? She's so wonderful and I think her

confidence is something I have to match. She has set the bar very high for a lot of woman. I need to be a confident woman and just say politically active things when I can that are helpful to young people.[157]

Although Lady Gaga's comments are ripe for misinterpretation, her message is an important one, even if her statement is slightly inaccurate. Adele has, of course, had her weight discussed in the prominent media repeatedly. But Lady Gaga's important point is that discussing a woman's weight on TV and, in particular, fat-shaming famous beautiful women, sets a terrible example for young people, making Adele's body positive statements all the more pressing and vital. While pitching herself against Adele in this way isn't the smartest move, it's valuable that famous women are discussing the scathing criticisms they regularly receive, incredibly publically, too. By challenging the issue, a pop star is able to draw attention back to the subject that should matter most: the music. Why are famous women being pitched against each other, and physically compared in this way?

Speaking to *Rolling Stone* in April 2011, Adele said,

My life is full of drama, and I don't have time to worry about something as petty as what I look like. I don't like going to the gym. I like eating fine foods and drinking nice wine. Even if I had a really good figure, I don't think I'd get my tits and ass out for no one. I love seeing Lady Gaga's boobs and bum. I love seeing Katy Perry's boobs and bum. Love it. But that's not what my music is about. I don't make music for eyes, I make music for ears."[158]

Adele's commitment to ensuring the focus is firmly on her music and not her body is further evidence that she's interested in establishing herself as a credible artist. By resisting the pressure to lose weight (though she has over the years, albeit gradually and for health reasons), Adele has continued to exercise self-love in the public eye. It's not easy taking a stand of this magnitude, but Adele has stuck to her guns, not listening to the criticisms about her weight, of which there are many.

Adele has always been a staunch advocate of body positivity. In an interview given in April 2008 to *The Telegraph*, Adele said, "If I wanted to be on the cover of *FHM*, then of course I'd be, like, fuck, I need to lose weight or, I need some fake tan or I need to get my teeth fixed. But I'd rather be on the cover of *Q* for my music."[159] This commitment to her music career over her image makes her role model material. In fact, for Adele, body image and mental health go hand in hand. In *The Telegraph*, Adele said, "If you ever see me rail thin, then you'll know there's something really wrong with me."[160] While her body positivity occasionally could be misconstrued as thin-shaming, liberally tarnishing female celebrities who happen to be very thin, Adele is consistently positive about one thing: herself. Adele's undying belief in her own abilities as a musician, and a strong attitude which refuses to acknowledge the ridiculous standards female pop stars are expected to adhere to, means that she's uninterested in being brought down by the small minds of others.

Does Adele have any cosmetic or fashion endorsements?

Adele once joked to Vogue magazine in October 2011 that if she was going to endorse anything, "it should be full-fat Coke!"[161] And it's Adele's enduring, and typically British, sense of humour that endears her to her many and varied fans. But despite having such a huge following, and being instantly recognisable across the globe, Adele has actually turned down many lucrative endorsements and deals.

In a profile in the *NY Times* by Jon Pareles, Adele said,

> If I wanted to just be famous, like be a celebrity, then I wouldn't do music, because everything else I've been offered would probably make me more famous than I am just with my music. Commercials, being the face of brands, nail varnishes, shoes, bags, fashion lines, beauty ranges, hair products, being in movies, being the face of a car, designing watches, food ranges, buildings, airlines, book deals. I've been offered everything. And I don't want to water myself down. I want to do one thing. I want to make something. I don't want to be the face of anything.[162]

Adele's insistence on being a musician, and not a celebrity, is valiant in a time when Taylor Swift is selling Keds, Katy Perry is promoting Pop Chips, and Beyonce is the face of high-profile brands like Pepsi and L'Oreal.[163] Whether Adele's stance will change now that album *25* has exploded, and with her burgeoning 2016 World Tour looming, is another matter. But at least for now, Adele continues to separate celebrity from music wherever possible.

Apparently demand for Adele is so real that companies have been offering her big-money deals for years. According to *The Sun* in March 2013, "Cosmetics giants including Estée Lauder, L'Oréal and Dior are fighting it out to make the singer the face of their skincare ranges."[164] According the *The Washinton Times*, L'Oreal were "left 'gobsmacked' after Adele reportedly walked away from a roughly $19 million (12 million pounds sterling) contract to be the makeup giant's new face."[165] Whether these rumours contained any truth or not, it certainly seems as though Adele is adamant to remain a musician and not dilute her image with sponsorship deals which don't relate to her music, even if they'd net her an inordinate amount of money.

Adele's stance has continued throughout the release of her new material and World Tour announcement in 2016. Claire Atkinson wrote for the *NY Post* in December 2015 that:

> So far there's no news on a tour sponsor, leading some to wonder if she doesn't want one. *The Post* had reported that her agents had been discussing a possible tie-up with Apple, but that crumbled for a variety of reasons, not least of which was the $30 million price tag, about three times what tours usually go for.[166]

While this sponsor didn't materialise, it looks as though Adele might have a price tag, for which she would allow a major endorsement deal to exist. However, the talk of Apple sponsoring the release of Adele's album and tour could be pure speculation. It certainly seems as though Adele isn't bothered in the slightest that her tour doesn't have a sponsorship deal, and her album has sold ridiculously well despite not being stocked in Apple stores.

To further confirm her disdain for sponsorship deals, speaking to *The Guardian* in November 2015, Adele said,

> What have I said no to? Everything you can imagine. Literally every-fucking-thing. Books, clothes, food ranges, drink ranges, fitness ranges... That's probably the funniest. They wanted me to be the face of a car. Toys. Apps. Candles. It's, like, I don't want to endorse a line of nail varnishes, but thanks for asking. A million pounds to sing at your birthday party? I'd rather do it for free if I'm doing it, cheers...[167]

Despite this claim, rumours continue to swirl that Adele will perform at Kate Middleton's birthday party,[168] for instance, and one would assume that's not a free gig, though it's probably an untrue claim. Aside from resisting a plethora of cosmetics and product endorsements and sponsorship deals,

Adele is also stern when it comes to her own albums, arguably the only products she *will* sell. As Adam Sherwin wrote in *The Independent*, "She won't tolerate the traditional marketing scam of record labels re-releasing albums with extra tracks to make fans buy a record twice."[169] Sherwin even quotes Adele on the issue, when she said, "I was furious when they did that on *19*. I said 'No' and they did it anyway. Just mugging off your fans."[170] It would seem now, though, that Adele is much more in control of her career and the decisions which go with it. It's certainly unusual to hear a pop star stand up against something the music industry does often – re-releasing an already successful album as a special edition with added extras, forcing fans to part with their money for a second time in order to own the upgrade. And, in her own way, Adele has already contradicted herself on this point with the release of *25*, as *The New York Times* said, "Target is the biggest driver of physical sales. The retailer had a special version of the album with three bonus songs, ran TV commercials promoting the release and placed cardboard displays filled with the CD by checkout lines."[171] While this has a lot to do with Adele's insistence on selling physical copies of her album, it seems suspect that the CD version of *25* has bonus songs that only people who buy this version can get hold of.

Although the legitimacy of magazine reports can't necessarily be trusted, people are still keen to pin endorsements to Adele, with everyone hoping she'd change her mind. Jack White wrote for *Closer Online* that, "It's been reported Adele, 27, is in the process of launching her own high street collection, which is said to be aimed at busy, working mums."[172] White cites *Now* who said, "It's still in the early stages, but she's been getting input from several designers and working on her own sketches. There will be a few signature pieces, like her favourite winter apparel, the poncho, but mostly it'll be mix-and-match daywear in neutral tones."[173] While this certainly sounds like exciting news that the demographic of Adele's fans would love, it still sounds dead against Adele's own stance on endorsing products. White continued, "If anyone knows what it's like to be a busy working mum, it's Adele."[174] While this is true, it seems far-fetched, though time will tell how far Adele will deviate from her previous point of view on the topic of celebrity sponsorships.

Adele has become a super successful pop star without compromising her image – how has she done it?

While pop stars often seem to be shoved into cookie-cutter moulds, making them exactly alike, Adele has resisted any such man-handling. Her willingness to be herself in the public eye is part of her charm, and makes her appear somewhat normal. Sure, she's super famous, and richer than most of us put together, but her attitude is always pretty chill. For instance, when Adele was interviewed by *The Telegraph* in 2008, relatively early in her career, she said, "I've never taken an illegal drug in my life. I want to be known for my music. I don't want to be in the press for having coke up my nose, because my nan will see it."[175] Despite the melancholic nature of her music, Adele's sense of humour is always intact, and it's her normal person approach to the music business that her kept her relatable. Describing Adele in *The Telegraph* back in 2008, Stuart Husband said, "Adele may be boisterous and larger than life, and have 'a serious cigarette and red wine habit', but she's no hell-raiser."[176] And if anything, since the early days of her success, Adele has dialled back any trace of party animal there once was.

One of the reasons Adele's managed to avoid compromising herself or her image is the normalcy with which she approaches the music industry and surrounding publicity. Speaking in *The Telegraph* in 2008, Adele said,

> I don't like photo sessions that much. That side of things is a lot harder than I thought it would be, in a good way, though. I mean, I never really thought about being a pop star, and I never thought about all the behind-the-scenes stuff that would come with it. I just thought I'd release a single and that would be that."[177]

The way in which Adele expresses surprise at dealing with the public side of the career she has chosen is interesting; her focus as always been firmly on the music, rather than being a pre-packaged pop star.

As Alexandra Shulman said in UK's *Vogue*, "Adele's very normality, her down-to-earth determination not to compromise herself, has become as much a part of her USP as, for example, Madonna's constant, deliberate reinvention."[178] Adele's strength, and unique selling point, as Shulman aptly puts it, is remaining steadfast in a world of ever-changing celebrities. In a world where being a chameleon is one of the highest compliments a person can be awarded, it's somewhat impressive that Adele's evolution has only taken place in the subject matter she's writing about, and only minor adjustments appear to have been made. After all, 'Hello', content-wise, does not sound all that different from Adele's previous releases. Which is no criticism – everything Adele has done, it clearly works.

What else should I know about Adele?

The one time Adele isn't afraid of the limelight is when she has an album due out. Then, out of necessity, she obligingly boards the publicity train and does all manner of TV performances, special previews, and personal interviews. When she's not touring or selling an album, Adele is all but off the map, often refusing publicity requests.

So, what are some of her best interviews, performances, photo shoots, and social media shares that you have to see, like, immediately? Here are just a few of the things you should seek out right now as a bona fide Adele fan.

Carpool Karaoke on The Late Late Show With James Corden

Adele took part in a special segment on James Corden's show in the US, in which the pair drove around in a car, singing along to songs from *25*, and hits by other people. Adele and Corden have worked together in the past, most notably when Corden hosted the BRIT Awards, famously cutting Adele's speech short in 2012, to which she swore at the crowd.[179]

About that Lionel Richie collaboration rumour...

It was inevitable that once someone created a mash-up of Adele's 'Hello' with Lionel Richie's 'Hello', talk of a duet between the two would start. While watching the mash-up itself is advised,[180] it was Richie's comments on the subject that were super interesting, particularly as some of his statements felt like a misguided attempt at humour. Speaking with *E! News*, Richie said, "You have no idea how many people called me on the phone and said, 'Are you going to let her get away with that? She stole 'Hello!'' Then I said I don't own 'Hello.' I own the melody."[181] Even though he seems pretty serious on the matter, hopefully Lionel Richie and friends all realise that *hello* is a pretty common word, and he doesn't own it. Still, Richie seems semi-convinced a legit collaboration between him and Adele could happen. He said, "We are going to be doing something together – that's already almost in the works... If I jump on her stage, she'd probably throw me out. Can you imagine 'Lionel Richie Jumps or Crawls Up on Adele's Stage?'"[182] At least he has a sense of humour about the whole thing, right?

Madame Tussauds

ITV reported in July 2013 that,

> After this year's Oscar and MBE, the multi-award winning singer and songwriter Adele has been honoured by Madame Tussauds, as wax figures of the acclaimed performer are revealed in London and Amsterdam. The figures will portray the singing sensation in a glamorous black dress, mirroring her Grammys 2012 look.[183]

Arguably one of the greatest honours a celebrity can receive, Adele now has waxworks in not just the London and Amsterdam branches of Madame Tussauds, but in San Francisco and New York, too.[184]

MBE

Adele was awarded an MBE in December 2013, for services to music. The Prince of Wales presented Adele with her award at Buckingham Palace.[185] It's possibly Adele's most impressive accolade.

Why did Adele quit drinking and smoking?

For years, Adele was adamant that she wouldn't give up cigarettes and alcohol. But as *Star Pulse* reported, Adele eventually spoke "about how doctors warned her about the smoking habit, that it would eventually cause chronic health problems. And even worse, continued smoking of 25 cigarettes a day could send her to an early grave."[186] The situation got even more serious, however, and in 2011, Adele was "undergoing surgery to repair chronic bleeding of her vocal chords."[187] *BBC America* reported via British *Glamour* and quoted Adele as having said,

> I gave up smoking for two months. It was fucking grim. I had laryngitis about a week before the album came out and it was so frightening. I stopped smoking, drinking, eating or drinking citrus, spicy foods and caffeine. It was so fucking boring... My

voice was better when I wasn't smoking. Within a week I noticed it had changed, but I'd rather my voice be a bit shit so I can have a fucking laugh."[188]

While Adele's insistence on enjoying her life is good to hear, her health appeared to be seriously at risk, and permanent damage to her throat looked possible, which would throw her singing career into jeopardy.

In 2015, Adele was open about her changed lifestyle. *Star Pulse* quoted Adele who said, "If I'd carried on smoking, I'd probably have died from a smoking-related illness, and I think that's really bad. If I was dying from lung cancer, I would have potentially given it to myself, and that wouldn't be something I'd be proud of." This complete U-turn is undoubtedly down to having had son, Angelo, and wanting to be able to provide for him. Adele may feel boring these days, but she's certainly healthier, and that's got to be a good thing.

I'm in love with Adele's bodyguard – is that normal?

As *Hollywood Life* announced, 'Adele's Bodyguard Is Super Hot & Everyone Is Freaking Out.'[189] And they didn't stop there. "Adele fans are demanding there be a remake of Whitney Houston's *The Bodyguard*, but this time around, they want the 'Hello' singer and her hunky bodyguard, Peter van der Veen, to star in it. Why? Because he's super hot and oh so sexy."[190] While his, y'know, skills as a bodyguard are probably way more important, the fact that the internet loves him doesn't hurt. *The Sun* did us all a major service when the compiled a mini biography of the bodyguard. Apparently, "he's well aware of his attractive appearance as he was crowned Mr Europe a decade ago. Blue-eyed Peter, who hails from Holland, made full use of his striking good looks by becoming a bodybuilder and flaunting his bulging muscles back in 2005."[191] Everyone's future husband sounds like a right catch.

Adele on breastfeeding

Despite being very private about her child, Adele has occasionally commented on motherhood. *The Guardian* described how, "In early 2013 she flew to Hollywood for the Globes and the Oscars, not so long after giving birth," with Adele herself joking how she was, "Running to the toilet, between awards, to pump-and-dump. Which loads of people were doing, by the way. All these Hollywood superstars, lined up and breastfeeding in the ladies. No, I can't say who. Because I saw their tits."[192] Motherhood has given Adele access to a famous mum's club, and in an age when public breastfeeding is still sometimes considered taboo, it's ace to hear Adele commenting so casually on the normality of it.

Adele's friend Alan Carr told *The Sun*,

> All I'll say is I have seen Adele's baby and he's such a cutie. She's doing great, she's glowing. Because we're friends, people will ask me on the red carpet if she's breast feeding or using a breast pump. Well I think that's fucking disgusting. This is a young girl, I'm not going to talk about her breasts."[193]

Even Adele's friends are fiercely protective of her privacy.

Adele on tattoos

A profile in *The New York Times* described some of Adele's body art, and said, "Tattooed along her right pinky is 'Angelo'; on her left pinky is 'Paradise' because, she explained, 'He's my paradise.'"[194] According to *Rolling Stone*, Adele has "a huge tattoo of three doves on her back."[195]

Adele also has an "A" tattooed on her neck, and an ellipsis tattooed on her wrist below a tattoo of a penny coin (her mum is called Penny).[196]

Why did Adele go undercover as an Adele impersonator?

In November 2015, Adele pulled off the best prank. She went undercover as an Adele impersonator and hung out with other Adele impersonators for the *BBC*.[197] *Entertainment Weekly* said, "To pull it off, Adele got a fake chin and fake nose to go undercover as Jenny, whose day job, Adele says, is nannying. When she introduces herself to the fellow impersonators, she does a pretty stellar job at hiding the fact that she does, in fact, have a casual ten Grammys at home. She even sneaks in a dig at herself and fakes some serious nerves before taking the stage."[198] Basically, Adele pulled off an epic prank that has to be seen, proving that she's not above making fun of herself, or meeting her fans.

People love Adele's Instagram that she took in the gym

Adele hit the gym at the start of 2016 in preparation for her World Tour. This, understandably, gave the public all the feels. In an article titled 'Why Adele's Workout Selfie Is This Week's Most Relatable Instagram', Calin Van Paris for *Vogue* wrote,

> Adele opted for a mock sob as she began her daily routine, a grimace with which even the most avid of exercisers can undoubtedly empathize. For those of us who experience a disconnect between saying we'll go to the gym and actually getting out of bed and going, Adele offers a new, more honest brand of motivation: Give yourself permission to whine, moan, and commiserate for a moment – and then work out anyway.[199]

As ever, Adele won over fans by appearing to be just like everyone else. Instead of presenting a so-called perfect celebrity persona, Adele uses honesty on social media.

CONCLUSION
THE FUTURE

What's next for Adele?

In March 2016, Adele embarks on a World Tour to accompany her album *25*. Following that, more singles are sure to follow. But what of the future?

Despite phenomenal success, Adele continues to be nervous about interest in her music, and is constantly questioning whether people will care what she does next. Health concerns also make her, understandably, anxious. In *Rolling Stone* in November 2015, Adele said, "I'll be able to get my throat fixed again and do studio work, but do I want to do something and then fail at it and be too scared to ever try it again?"[200] Fear of failure seems to plague Adele, however high she reaches.

Adele's future is sure to be amazing. Speaking to *Apple Music*, Adele said, "*25* is the perfect age to end the albums named after my age,"[201] making this a very special era that we're in. Adele's trilogy of albums may have come to an end, but the future is filled with possibility. Whatever Adele chooses to do next – more albums, tours, movie roles, or long-awaited ad campaigns – the fans will most definitely be waiting.

ABOUT THE AUTHOR

Amy Mackelden is an Entertainment Writer for *Bustle* and a pop culture blogger at *Clarissa Explains Fuck All*. She's written for *Heat, New Statesman, The Independent* online, *Hello Giggles, xoJane, Kinkly,* and *Writing in Education*. She co-founded *Butcher's Dog* poetry magazine, and is developing a theatre show called *MS is my Boyfriend*, about life with multiple sclerosis.

Thanks to:
Laura Hol for taking my photo and defending me from the squirrels.
Todd Swift for saying yes to my cray pitch!
Dylan Jaggard for being bae. And, y'know, editing and shit.

ENDNOTES

1 http://www.billboard.com/articles/news/6745062/adele-hello-biggest-youtube-debut-this-year

2 http://www.telegraph.co.uk/culture/music/3672957/Adele-young-soul-rebel.html

3 http://mic.com/articles/120804/the-story-behind-how-adele-became-the-defining-british-artist-of-the-2010s#.CePDVXNj1

4 http://mic.com/articles/120804/the-story-behind-how-adele-became-the-defining-british-artist-of-the-2010s#.CePDVXNj1

5 http://www.telegraph.co.uk/culture/music/3672957/Adele-young-soul-rebel.html

6 http://www.brit.croydon.sch.uk/

7 http://www.capitalfm.com/artists/jessie-j/news/adele-friend-brit-school-autobiography/#IeDDryiwWfvMaCDS.97

8 http://www.croydonadvertiser.co.uk/BRIT-School-music-teacher-knew-Adele-star/story-18155425-detail/story.html#ixzz3xdBCrVoX

9 http://www.telegraph.co.uk/culture/music/3672957/Adele-young-soul-rebel.html

10 http://www.telegraph.co.uk/culture/music/3672957/Adele-young-soul-rebel.html

11 http://www.lifetimetv.co.uk/biography/biography-adele

12 http://www.telegraph.co.uk/culture/music/3672957/Adele-young-soul-rebel.html

13 http://www.telegraph.co.uk/culture/music/8430164/Adele-shes-stopped-us-in-her-tracks.html

14 http://www.telegraph.co.uk/culture/music/3672957/Adele-young-soul-rebel.html

15 http://www.telegraph.co.uk/culture/music/3672957/Adele-young-soul-rebel.html

16 http://www.telegraph.co.uk/culture/music/8430164/Adele-shes-stopped-us-in-her-tracks.html

17 http://www.theguardian.com/music/2015/nov/15/adele-25-new-album-interview

18 http://www.bbc.co.uk/music/reviews/6pf9

19 http://www.slantmagazine.com/music/review/adele-19

20 http://www.theguardian.com/music/2008/jan/20/popandrock.shopping1

21 http://www.bbc.co.uk/music/reviews/6pf9

22 http://www.bbc.co.uk/music/reviews/6pf9

23 http://www.allmusic.com/artist/adele-mn0000503460/discography/singles

24 http://www.pacemakerrecordings.com/

25 http://www.theguardian.com/music/2008/jan/20/popandrock.shopping1

26 http://www.theguardian.com/music/2015/mar/19/adeles-21-is-the-best-selling-uk-album-of-the-millenium

27 http://www.officialcharts.com/chart-news/official-biggest-selling-albums-of-the-millennium-so-far-revealed-__8698/

28 http://www.nytimes.com/2015/11/15/arts/music/adele-25-album-interview.html?_r=1
29 http://www.nytimes.com/2015/11/15/arts/music/adele-25-album-interview.html?_r=1
30 http://www.nytimes.com/2015/11/15/arts/music/adele-25-album-interview.html?_r=1
31 http://www.nytimes.com/2015/11/15/arts/music/adele-25-album-interview.html?_r=1
32 http://www.billboard.com/biz/articles/news/1177102/adeles-rolling-in-the-deep-is-the-biggest-crossover-song-of-past-25-years
33 http://mic.com/articles/120804/the-story-behind-how-adele-became-the-defining-british-artist-of-the-2010s#.CePDVXNj1
34 http://www.theguardian.com/music/2015/nov/19/adele-25-album-review
35 http://www.theguardian.com/music/2015/nov/19/adele-25-album-review
36 http://pitchfork.com/reviews/albums/21246-25/
37 http://www.theguardian.com/music/2015/nov/19/adele-25-album-review
38 http://pitchfork.com/reviews/albums/21246-25/
39 http://www.telegraph.co.uk/music/what-to-listen-to/adele-25-review/
40 http://www.telegraph.co.uk/music/what-to-listen-to/adele-25-review/
41 https://www.youtube.com/watch?v=DDWKuo3gXMQ
42 http://www.billboard.com/articles/columns/chart-beat/6806119/adele-when-we-were-young-second-single-25
43 http://www.bbc.co.uk/news/entertainment-arts-34808865
44 http://www.bbc.co.uk/news/entertainment-arts-21570148
45 http://www.billboard.com/articles/news/474103/amas-2012-full-winners-list
46 http://web.archive.org/web/20120705065452/http://www.billboard.com/bbma/winners
47 http://www.independent.co.uk/arts-entertainment/music/news/brit-awards-winners-2013-the-list-in-full-8504404.html
48 http://www.telegraph.co.uk/culture/music/music-news/8337781/Adele-soars-to-top-of-charts-after-Brits-performance.html
49 http://variety.com/2012/music/news/adele-s-21-wins-album-of-the-year-at-grammys-1118050159/
50 http://www.theguardian.com/music/2012/apr/17/adele-ivor-novello-awards
51 http://www.mtv.com/ontv/vma/2011/
52 http://www.billboard.com/articles/columns/pop-shop/6738256/adele-albums-age
53 http://www.billboard.com/articles/columns/pop-shop/6738256/adele-albums-age
54 http://www.bluesandsoul.com/feature/302/the_futures_looking_rosie_for_adele/
55 http://www.billboard.com/articles/columns/pop-shop/6738256/adele-albums-age

56 http://www.thesun.co.uk/sol/homepage/showbiz/6778844/After-releasing-19-21-and-25-Adele-hints-that-next-album-could-be-seven-years-away.html

57 http://www.bluesandsoul.com/feature/302/adele__up_close_and_personal/

58 http://www.telegraph.co.uk/culture/music/3672957/Adele-young-soul-rebel.html

59 http://www.telegraph.co.uk/culture/music/3672957/Adele-young-soul-rebel.html

60 http://americansongwriter.com/2012/01/the-story-behind-the-song-adele-someone-like-you/

61 http://americansongwriter.com/2012/01/the-story-behind-the-song-adele-someone-like-you/

62 http://www.amazon.co.uk/Live-Royal-Albert-incl-Region/dp/B005Z4D26U/ref=sr_1_1?ie=UTF8&qid=1452956518&sr=8-1&keywords=adele+royal+albert

63 http://www.amazon.co.uk/Live-Royal-Albert-incl-Region/dp/B005Z4D26U/ref=sr_1_1?ie=UTF8&qid=1452956518&sr=8-1&keywords=adele+royal+albert

64 http://www.bustle.com/articles/119205-6-fierce-adele-quotes-what-we-can-learn-from-them

65 https://www.youtube.com/watch?v=Zp8BZQc6hVQ

66 http://www.rollingstone.com/music/news/adele-talks-25-hello-origins-and-darkness-in-new-interviews-20151023#ixzz3xDa6naE1

67 http://www.telegraph.co.uk/culture/music/8430164/Adele-shes-stopped-us-in-her-tracks.html

68 https://www.youtube.com/watch?v=DDWKuo3gXMQ

69 https://www.youtube.com/watch?v=-xJrcWtM6jQ

70 https://www.youtube.com/watch?v=if2jzYisu7Q

71 https://www.youtube.com/watch?v=xNP0Nxf7E8A

72 http://www.theguardian.com/music/2015/nov/15/adele-25-new-album-interview

73 http://www.theguardian.com/music/2015/nov/15/adele-25-new-album-interview

74 http://www.amazon.co.uk/So-Called-Chaos-Alanis-Morissette/dp/B0001MDP40

75 http://www.amazon.co.uk/So-Called-Chaos-Alanis-Morissette/dp/B0001MDP40

76 http://www.vulture.com/2012/10/who-is-each-song-on-taylor-swifts-album-about.html

77 http://nypost.com/2012/02/12/rolling-with-the-creep/

78 http://www.telegraph.co.uk/news/celebritynews/9182626/Adeles-mystery-ex-revealed-claims-magazine.html

79 http://www.telegraph.co.uk/news/celebritynews/9182626/Adeles-mystery-ex-revealed-claims-magazine.html

80 http://www.dailymail.co.uk/femail/article-3280773/Who-ex-Adele-just-t-forget-Latest-song-lyrics-inspired-doomed-romance-mystery-man.html#ixzz3xPbXtunX

81 http://time.com/4155795/adele-time-cover-story-interview-motherhood-25/

82 http://www.theguardian.com/music/2015/oct/19/adele-teases-with-new-song-in-x-factor-ad-break-and-internet-melts

83 http://www.vocativ.com/news/272360/adele-takes-over-youtube-shattering-yet-another-record/

84 http://youtube-trends.blogspot.co.uk/2015/10/adeles-new-single-played-over-1m.html

85 http://www.bustle.com/articles/119190-adeles-hello-breaks-vevo-record-proving-the-soulful-singer-is-still-at-the-top-of-her

86 https://www.youtube.com/watch?v=YQHsXMglC9A

87 http://www.bustle.com/articles/135000-adele-james-corden-do-carpool-karaoke-in-this-hilarious-teaser-for-the-upcoming-episode

88 http://www.ew.com/article/2015/10/26/adele-hello-tristan-mack-wilds

89 http://www.ew.com/article/2015/10/26/adele-hello-tristan-mack-wilds

90 http://www.ew.com/article/2015/10/26/adele-hello-tristan-mack-wilds

91 http://www.ew.com/article/2015/10/26/adele-hello-tristan-mack-wilds

92 http://abcnews.go.com/Entertainment/actor-tristan-wilds-reflects-starring-adeles-music-video/story?id=35844569

93 http://www.comingsoon.net/extras/trailers/625429-adeles-hello-video-imax

94 http://abcnews.go.com/Entertainment/actor-tristan-wilds-reflects-starring-adeles-music-video/story?id=35844569

95 http://abcnews.go.com/Entertainment/actor-tristan-wilds-reflects-starring-adeles-music-video/story?id=35844569

96 http://thefeminismproject.com/entertainment/adeles-new-video-features-beautiful-interracial-loving-and-epic-eyeliner/

97 http://abcnews.go.com/Entertainment/shonda-rhimes-talks-strong-women-weak-men-setting/story?id=25582749

98 https://medium.com/@new_girl_friday/adele-s-interracial-relationship-in-hello-video-is-more-important-than-you-think-ce3f23bc3746#.nvioyho7c

99 https://medium.com/@new_girl_friday/adele-s-interracial-relationship-in-hello-video-is-more-important-than-you-think-ce3f23bc3746#.nvioyho7c

100 http://m.fafmag.com/entertainment/adele-video-has-interracial-couple/

101 http://abcnews.go.com/Entertainment/actor-tristan-wilds-reflects-starring-adeles-music-video/story?id=35844569

102 https://twitter.com/Adele/status/667703151965904896

103 http://www.rollingstone.com/music/news/adele-inside-her-private-life-and-triumphant-return-20151103#ixzz3wDlIH5yH

104 http://www.rollingstone.com/music/news/adele-inside-her-private-life-and-triumphant-return-20151103#ixzz3wDlIH5yH

105 http://www.billboard.com/articles/columns/pop-shop/6714457/sia-alive-adele-jesse-shatkin-interview
106 http://www.billboard.com/articles/columns/pop-shop/6714457/sia-alive-adele-jesse-shatkin-interview
107 http://www.theguardian.com/music/2015/nov/03/adele-i-regret-working-with-damon-albarn
108 https://twitter.com/Adele/status/656787881349009408
109 https://twitter.com/Adele/status/656787881349009408
110 http://time.com/4155586/adele-time-cover-story-interview-streaming/
111 http://www.theguardian.com/music/2014/nov/04/taylor-swift-spotify-streaming-album-sales-snub
112 http://time.com/4155586/adele-time-cover-story-interview-streaming/
113 spotify:album:7n3QJc7TBOxXtlYh4Ssll8
114 https://www.facebook.com/adele/videos/10153534517994279/
115 http://www.bustle.com/articles/129200-adele-is-setting-an-amazing-example-for-artists-with-ticket-sales-for-her-upcoming-tour
116 http://www.independent.co.uk/arts-entertainment/music/news/adele-saves-fans-4m-by-taking-tour-tickets-out-of-the-hands-of-touts-a6767316.html
117 https://twitter.com/Adele/status/676371435611377664
118 http://live.adele.com/
119 http://www.theatlantic.com/business/archive/2015/12/adele-scalpers/421362/
120 https://twitter.com/the_alyssa_noll
121 http://time.com/4155795/adele-time-cover-story-interview-motherhood-25/
122 http://time.com/4155795/adele-time-cover-story-interview-motherhood-25/
123 http://www.theguardian.com/music/2015/nov/03/adele-i-regret-working-with-damon-albarn
124 http://time.com/4155795/adele-time-cover-story-interview-motherhood-25/
125 http://www.telegraph.co.uk/culture/music/3672957/Adele-young-soul-rebel.html
126 http://time.com/4155795/adele-time-cover-story-interview-motherhood-25/
127 http://time.com/4155795/adele-time-cover-story-interview-motherhood-25/
128 http://edition.cnn.com/2015/11/23/entertainment/adele-hello-25-feat/
129 http://edition.cnn.com/2015/11/23/entertainment/adele-hello-25-feat/
130 http://www.capitalfm.com/artists/robbie-williams/news/america-success/
131 http://www.telegraph.co.uk/music/artists/what-happened-to-daniel-and-natasha-bedingfield/
132 http://www.digitalspy.com/showbiz/news/a321419/adele-tax-bill-made-her-want-to-buy-a-gun-and-open-fire/
133 http://www.digitalspy.com/showbiz/news/a321419/adele-tax-bill-made-her-want-to-buy-a-gun-and-open-fire/
134 http://blogs.telegraph.co.uk/news/willheaven/100089687/dont-worry-adele-the-telegraphs-got-your-back/
135 http://www.theguardian.com/music/musicblog/2011/may/25/adele-tax-grievances

136 http://www.nydailynews.com/entertainment/gossip/singer-adele-sparks-online-backlash-complaining-paying-taxes-article-1.127662

137 http://www.theguardian.com/music/2015/nov/15/adele-25-new-album-interview

138 http://www.nytimes.com/2015/11/15/arts/music/adele-25-album-interview.html?_r=0

139 http://www.theguardian.com/music/2015/nov/15/adele-25-new-album-interview

140 http://www.theguardian.com/media/2014/jul/23/adele-son-payout-privacy-corbis-angelo-adkins

141 http://fortune.com/2015/11/07/adele-hello-marketing-machine/

142 http://www.rollingstone.com/music/news/adele-inside-her-private-life-and-triumphant-return-20151103

143 http://www.rollingstone.com/music/news/adele-inside-her-private-life-and-triumphant-return-20151103

144 https://soundcloud.com/siriusxmmusic/sets/adele-speaks-with-the-spectrums-jenny-eliscu-for-a-siriusxm-town-hall

145 http://www.billboard.com/articles/news/6786002/adele-grammys-not-nominated

146 http://adele.wikia.com/wiki/Daydreamers

147 http://www.usatoday.com/story/life/entertainthis/2015/10/23/adele-released-hello-new-song-from-her-album-25-tristan-wilds-flip-phones/74447124/

148 http://www.nytimes.com/2015/11/28/business/media/adele-shatters-music-industry-truisms-by-going-against-the-grain.html?smprod=nytcore-iphone&smid=nytcore-iphone-share

149 http://www.nytimes.com/2015/11/28/business/media/adele-shatters-music-industry-truisms-by-going-against-the-grain.html?smprod=nytcore-iphone&smid=nytcore-iphone-share

150 http://www.nytimes.com/2015/11/28/business/media/adele-shatters-music-industry-truisms-by-going-against-the-grain.html?smprod=nytcore-iphone&smid=nytcore-iphone-share

151 http://www.nytimes.com/2015/11/28/business/media/adele-shatters-music-industry-truisms-by-going-against-the-grain.html?smprod=nytcore-iphone&smid=nytcore-iphone-share

152 https://soundcloud.com/siriusxmmusic/sets/adele-speaks-with-the-spectrums-jenny-eliscu-for-a-siriusxm-town-hall

153 http://www.huffingtonpost.com/2013/03/29/joan-rivers-on-adele-shes_n_2981229.html

154 http://www.huffingtonpost.com/2013/03/29/joan-rivers-on-adele-shes_n_2981229.html

155 http://www.theguardian.com/fashion/fashion-blog/2012/feb/08/karl-lagerfeld-adele

156 http://www.vogue.co.uk/news/2011/09/05/october-issue-of-vogue---adele/

157 http://www.stylist.co.uk/beauty/the-passion-of-lady-gaga#art

158 http://www.rollingstone.com/music/news/adele-opens-up-about-her-inspirations-looks-and-stage-fright-20120210?page=3

159 http://www.telegraph.co.uk/culture/music/3672957/Adele-young-soul-rebel.html

160 http://www.telegraph.co.uk/culture/music/3672957/Adele-young-soul-rebel.html

161 http://www.vogue.co.uk/news/2011/09/05/october-issue-of-vogue---adele/

162 http://www.nytimes.com/2015/11/15/arts/music/adele-25-album-interview.html?_r=0

163 http://www.forbes.com/sites/meghancasserly/2012/12/10/beyonce-knowles-50-million-pepsi-deal-takes-creative-cues-from-jay-z/

164 http://www.thesun.co.uk/sol/homepage/showbiz/bizarre/4840588/Cosmetics-companies-battle-for-Adele.html

165 http://www.washingtontimes.com/news/2013/nov/10/loreal-godsmacked-after-adele-turns-down-19-millio/

166 http://nypost.com/2015/12/19/adele-doesnt-seem-interested-in-sponsors-for-massive-tour/

167 http://www.theguardian.com/music/2015/nov/15/adele-25-new-album-interview

168 https://uk.news.yahoo.com/adele-perform-kate-middletons-birthday-095525546.html

169 http://www.independent.co.uk/arts-entertainment/music/news/the-secret-of-adeles-success-no-festivals-tweeting-ndash-or-selling-out-2288168.html

170 http://www.independent.co.uk/arts-entertainment/music/news/the-secret-of-adeles-success-no-festivals-tweeting-ndash-or-selling-out-2288168.html

171 http://www.nytimes.com/2015/11/28/business/media/adele-shatters-music-industry-truisms-by-going-against-the-grain.html?smprod=nytcore-iphone&smid=nytcore-iphone-share

172 http://www.closeronline.co.uk/2016/01/adele-style-fashion-collection

173 http://www.closeronline.co.uk/2016/01/adele-style-fashion-collection

174 http://www.closeronline.co.uk/2016/01/adele-style-fashion-collection

175 http://www.telegraph.co.uk/culture/music/3672957/Adele-young-soul-rebel.html

176 http://www.telegraph.co.uk/culture/music/3672957/Adele-young-soul-rebel.html

177 http://www.telegraph.co.uk/culture/music/3672957/Adele-young-soul-rebel.html

178 http://www.vogue.co.uk/news/2011/09/05/october-issue-of-vogue---adele/

179 https://www.youtube.com/watch?v=q7aDyR1mXog

180 http://www.bustle.com/articles/119006-what-would-an-adele-lionel-richie-hello-collaboration-sound-like

181 http://www.eonline.com/uk/news/720152/lionel-richie-reveals-plans-for-upcoming-collaboration-with-adele-after-mashup-of-hello-goes-viral?cmpid=rss-000000-rssfeed-365-topstories&utm_source=eonline&utm_medium=rssfeeds&utm_campaign=rss_topstories

182 http://www.eonline.com/uk/news/720152/lionel-richie-reveals-plans-for-upcoming-collaboration-with-adele-after-mashup-of-hello-goes-viral?cmpid=rss-000000-rssfeed-365-topstories&utm_source=eonline&utm_medium=rssfeeds&utm_campaign=rss_topstories

183 http://www.itv.com/news/london/2013-07-03/adele-waxwork-joins-madame-tussauds-hall-of-fame/

184 https://www2.madametussauds.com/san-francisco/en/whats-inside/music-zone/adele/

185 http://www.bbc.co.uk/news/entertainment-arts-25452604

186 http://www.starpulse.com/news/index.php/2015/12/20/fearing-death-adele-stopped-smoking-dr

187 http://www.starpulse.com/news/index.php/2015/12/20/fearing-death-adele-stopped-smoking-dr

188 http://www.bbcamerica.com/shows//blog/2011/06/quit-smoking-not-a-chance-says-adele

189 http://hollywoodlife.com/2015/11/27/adele-bodyguard-hot-peter-van-der-veen-fans-react-twitter/

190 http://hollywoodlife.com/2015/11/27/adele-bodyguard-hot-peter-van-der-veen-fans-react-twitter/

191 http://www.thesun.co.uk/sol/homepage/showbiz/bizarre/celebs/adele/6776341/Revealed-The-secret-past-of-Adeles-hunky-bodyguard-Peter-Van-der-Veen.html

192 http://www.theguardian.com/music/2015/nov/15/adele-25-new-album-interview

193 http://www.thesun.co.uk/sol/homepage/features/4651596/Alan-Carr-secrets-of-interviewing-likes-of-Westlife-and-Lady-Gaga.html

194 http://www.nytimes.com/2015/11/15/arts/music/adele-25-album-interview.html?_r=1

195 http://www.rollingstone.com/music/news/adele-inside-her-private-life-and-triumphant-return-20151103#ixzz3xhjS3scq

196 http://adele.wikia.com/wiki/Tattoos

197 https://www.youtube.com/watch?v=OHXjxWaQs9o

198 http://www.ew.com/article/2015/11/20/adele-impersonated-adele-impersonator-bbc-prank

199 http://www.vogue.com/13384971/adele-workout-selfie-new-years-resolutions-fitness/

200 http://www.rollingstone.com/music/news/adele-inside-her-private-life-and-triumphant-return-20151103#ixzz3xi702c00

201 http://www.rollingstone.com/music/news/adele-talks-25-hello-origins-and-darkness-in-new-interviews-20151023#ixzz3xi7uYLJP

INDEX

EYEWEAR PUBLISHING

we are an independent press
based in London, England.
Emphasis is on excellent new
work, in poetry and prose. Our
range is international and our
aim is true. Look into some of the
most stylish books around today.